# BURMA
# THE GOLDEN

*Photography by Günter Pfannmüller*

*Text by Wilhelm Klein*

*Design Direction by Vilibald Barl*

# BURMA
## THE GOLDEN

Published by
Höfer Media (Pte) Ltd 1995
ISBN 962-421-188-4
Printed in Singapore
by Höfer Press (Pte) Ltd
*All Rights Reserved*

# *Contents*

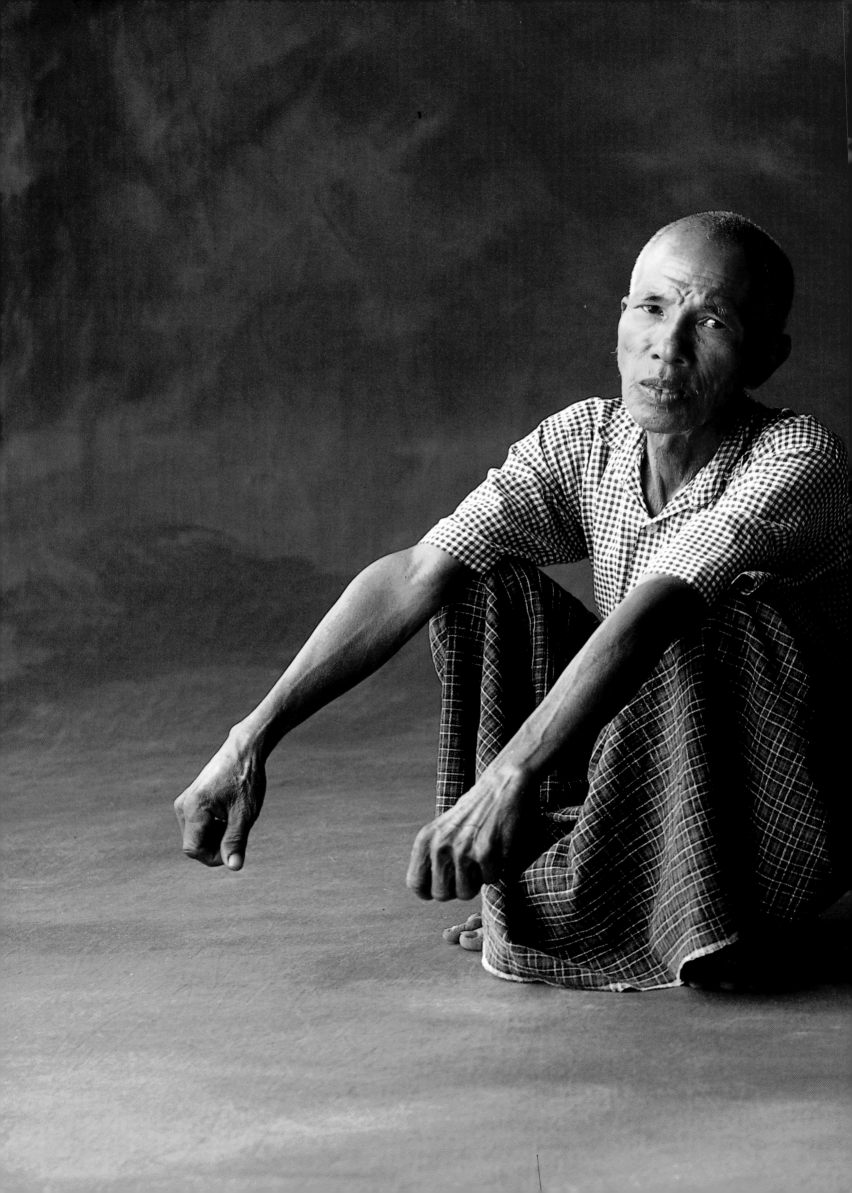

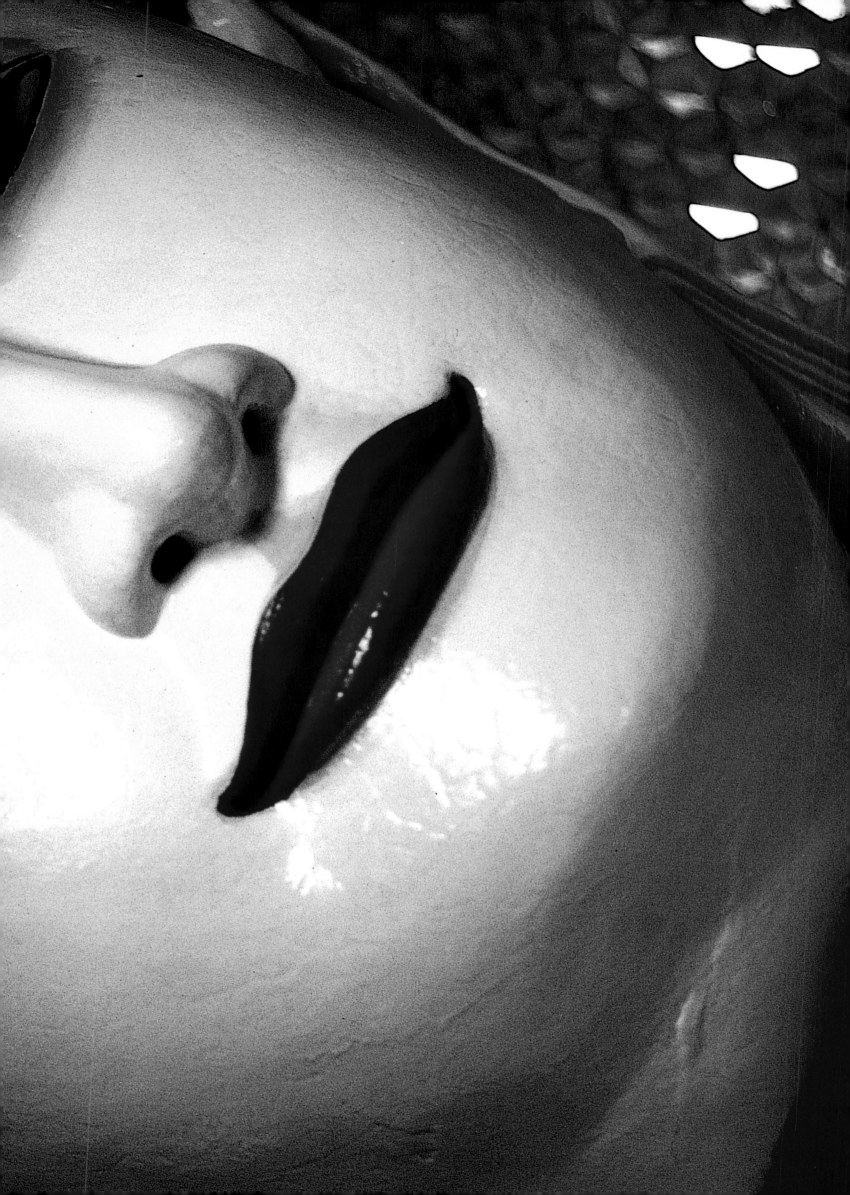

**Y**e dhamma heturprabhava …
The Buddha hath the causes told
of all things springing from causes;
And also how things cease to be,
'tis this the Mighty Monk proclaims.
*The Buddhist creed.*

**T**raveling through Myanmar is unlike traveling through any other country in the world. Besides its gentle people and its breathtaking views, Myanmar offers a journey through a landscape that is beyond the scope of our senses. It is a journey through an astounding reality but one that surprises the traveler with uniquely metaphysical scenes that can occur at any time in any place. In this book, we hope to portray what particularly inspires us about Myanmar: a country where the values and ideas of the past are still vividly present beneath a veil of modern concepts.

*A product of history.* This book will acquaint you with a most intricate cultural environment. While the rest of the world has marched steadfastly down a one-way road towards economic progress, Myanmar has remained isolated from Western thought for an extraordinarily long time and the peculiar lifestyle of its people is the result of this seclusion. Only very recently, historically speaking, during the Konbaung dynasty that ended in 1885, the presence of the royal court was the guarantor and the proof of the *dhamma*, the Buddhist law. All buildings, royal or ecclesiastical, reflected an otherwise invisible reality; they were built to illustrate the many planes of existence that the people believed thrived around them.

The British colonial period may have lasted 123 years in South Myanmar and 62 years in the north, but it didn't change the beliefs of the indigenous people, as they employed mostly Muslim and Hindu Indians to govern and exploit the country. Meanwhile, the Myanmars stuck to their ancient way of life and remained paddy farmers. Those British officials, scholars and civil servants who have written about their experiences during that era have left us a treasure of literature and a portrait of a people enshrouded in myths and superstitions.

Unfiltered Western thought penetrated the country only for a very short period in the 1950s. Soon, however, in the year 1962, after 14 years of independence, the country was on the brink of breaking up. Continuous civil unrest and an unsuccessful period of democratic rule by U Nu led to a bloodless coup by the *tatmadaw*, the military. Between 1962 and 1974, General Ne Win ruled Myanmar by decree and foreigners were only permitted in on official missions. After the implementation of a socialist constitution and a one-party system, a small window opened to the outside world and, with the seven-day visiting permits, a quite short period commenced during which an adventurous traveler could get more than just a glimpse of the country's hidden wealth. This was the time when *Burma the Golden* left its mark on almost every visitor. Though traveling within the country was still severely restricted, one could get by. Proverbial Myanmar hospitality and Buddhist goodwill was extended to everyone, revealing a world which otherwise was hidden behind political paroles and restrictions.

After the political turmoil of 1988, traveling in Myanmar became again difficult; individual travelers were not permitted and all groups were accompanied by guides. Since 1994, this has, however, drastically changed. The need for foreign exchange has initiated a new, more liberal policy. Now, one can stay for four weeks and this period can be extended for another four weeks without difficulties. Individual travelers are welcome again. With the new constitution implemented, one which is supposed to be similar to the Indonesian one, and an abating of the civil war, yet untouched regions will be opened to visitors. A world that seemed to have vanished in the turmoil of this century will thus become visible again. Only time will show how much the foreseeable influx of travelers will affect the uniqueness of the place.

*Mythical Myanmar.* If myths are humanity's earliest answers to the mysteries of life, then an unhampered journey through Myanmar, a country that is still enveloped in

myths, as if in a cocoon, will lead you to some of humanity's most beautiful mythological manifestations. In this book, it is our intention to capture in words and pictures, some of the many facets that the country reveals to the inquisitive mind. Enticed
and enmeshed by Buddhist stories and concepts, we have attempted to catch a glimpse
of a world that is normally shrouded by the trivial face of everyday life, and by facts
that are presented with statistical accuracy. Both elements work like a filter and only
by avoiding their distorting message can you see the other face of the country. In
Myanmar, people live in a community where the pragmatic and pious wisdom of their
forefathers is still very present. We have visited Myanmar for years, comparing the
mythical with the rational, and in this book we try to share the charm and enchant-
ment that is so overwhelming and otherworldly.

The key component of Myanmar's charm is its unique form of Buddhism. It distin-
guishes the people of the Ayeyarwady valley from most other Southeast Asians. Here,
ethereal realms and fables of Theravada Buddhism have merged with ancient animistic *nat*-worship. The mind boggles with fairy-tale visions, and Myanmar's idyllic
landscape acts to feed that imagination, as it is dotted everywhere with remarkable
stupas, temples and monasteries.

*A way of coping.* In sharp contrast to this living fantasy, the Myanmar people,
while believing in doctrines formulated 25 centuries ago, lead a rather harsh existence. In terms of its GNP, Myanmar is one of the poorest countries in the world.
There is no immediate prospect of a purely civilian government and the armed conflict with the communities and tribes that live in the mountains around the Ayeyarwady valley seems to be unending. Thus, in spite of the gentleness that Buddhism
promotes, Myanmar is far from being a haven of peace and tranquillity. Most Myanmars only manage to face this protracted situation through their staunch belief in
Buddhist precepts. Indeed, the pious Buddhist sees earthly attainment as a waste of
energy. For him, his lifetime is only one of an endless number of miserable existences
in which he can do nothing but refine his *kamma* (*karma* in Sanskrit). One day, after
innumerable rebirths, his *kamma* might lead him to *nibbana* (*nirvana* in Sanskrit),
but he knows he cannot expect it after only this life.

*Snarled in contradictions.* This Buddhist belief is itself a myth to most Westerners.
It clashes with the modern view that this life is the only known quantity, therefore
happiness should be sought now, through rational and science-oriented living. Buddhists refute this outlook with their own brand of science; they say the main experience of life will always be *dukkha*, suffering. They say that modern science cannot
overcome it, being itself a vulnerable product of *anicca*, impermanence. While trying
to document at least something of the basic contradiction underlying the reality of
modern Myanmar, we realized that we had to penetrate the country on different levels. A horizontal study of Myanmar catches its geography and its visual truth, while
a vertical view reveals the historic development of the nation, its racial diversity, its
religious expressions and the artistic traditions handed down by generations long
since gone. Together they form the background that helps to explain some of the otherwise incomprehensible accounts we read of the country today. Myanmar's show-
places of history are dispersed all over the country. Its kings' habit of shifting their
capitals periodically, and the choice of regions where the diverse tribes settled, have
given us the opportunity to weave in geographical sights with historical and philo-
sophical reflections in the pages which follow. It was only after acquainting ourselves
thoroughly with the religious background of the people that we set out to try to
unravel some of Myanmar's myths. Soon, however, we discovered that the more we
tried to do so, the more we became entangled in its seductive beauty, snarled up in a
lifestyle so different from ours.

*The journey.* This book follows a rather unusual method of penetrating an alien culture. The first chapter, *Landscapes of the Mind*, will acquaint you with the way the Myanmars see themselves and their homeland; then, the chapters on Bagan (Pagan) and Mandalay focus on the historical heritage that is so important to the patriotism of these seemingly self-sufficient people. In the chapters *Rakhine* and *Inle*, some of the peripheral influences that contribute to the magic of Myanmar are explained, and finally in *Ramanadesa*, the chapter about South Myanmar, the circle that began with *Suvannabhumi*, the "Golden Land" of lore, and ends with today's *Burma the Golden* is completed. Words cannot suffice to fathom the essence of a country as culturally and geographically diversified as Myanmar. Myanmar is strikingly picturesque, a feast for the eye; but it takes all our senses to understand the links that exist between the natural beauty and the manmade environment, between the beauty of the metaphysical dome and the architectural remnants that span the chronological history as well as the vast landscape of the country.

For those who are not yet accustomed to calling this country Myanmar but still use the former name *Burma*, many names and the way they are written in this book will seem strange. Since 1989, however, not only the country has changed its official name, but also many of its cities and rivers. In spite of these changes we have titled this book Burma, since the hidden charm of the country has become known under this name in Western media. The old names we know were actually the written version of the British pronounciation of Myanmar words. A decree by the SLORC has now changed all these names for good. Rangoon became Yangon, Pagan changed to Bagan, Pegu to Bago, Moulmein to Mawlamyine, Bassein to Pathein, Prome to Pyay and Maymyo to Pyin-U-Lwin. Tenasserim became Tanintharyi and Arakan changed to Rakhine. Of the rivers, the Irrawaddy became the Ayeyarwady and the Salween changed its name to Thanlwin. Though many will look back with regret to the old familiar colonial names, this is one way the Myanmars want to keep control of their own history, demonstrating that the British period was just a short interlude in historical terms. It's a small contribution to the drive to revive the ancient Myanmar way of life and to bar Western influences wherever possible.

There are books that describe the economic or political hardship this country is experiencing. This book just tries to show you some of its hidden splendor, its endangered way of life, that the sensitive, individual traveler will surely cherish, but which cannot survive if trampled upon by millions of tourists who in their heart of hearts do not really care. Neither does this book ask if the policy of isolation from cosmopolitan ideas is a legitimate one in the 20th century. Instead, the book is intended to serve only one purpose: to be a snapshot of a constantly changing world, documenting some of the vanishing charms of a lifestyle which has elsewhere already gone forever.

*Myths are everywhere.* One typical unreal night, during one of our journeys to Myanmar, we were sitting on top of the U Min Kyaukse Pagoda overlooking Sagaing, listening to *pongyis* (monks) chanting from Pali scriptures. We realized that the myths surrounding this ancient land could not be rationalized – that to try to demystify what has grown for millennia is like watching sand disappear between your fingers: just when you think you have focused on a constant stream, you see that there is nothing left to describe, that nothing remains that is lasting, that everything is in a state of flux. Buddhist law is built on that revelation. That night, we watched with reverence as the perennially flowing Ayeyarwady dawdled beneath a starlit sky. The voices of the *pongyis* drifting up to our pagoda platform somehow seemed to weave heaven and earth together. There and then a new thought arose in our Western minds: perhaps the many scientific answers we get to the as yet unanswered cosmic puzzle are also no more than myths themselves – modern ones, perhaps, but myths nonetheless.

# LANDSCAPES OF THE MIND

*The Cosmography of the Theravadins*

There are many angles from which to look at one and the same topic. Each produces a certain set of emotions that derives from its particular view, and when used in a religious context, could lead to a fundamentalist stance. This applies in Myanmar just as it does anywhere else. The Myanmar's system of perceiving reality is a complex and all-encompassing one, but it should not be foreign to us because our scientific views belong to the same category.

For the pious Buddhist, the source of all knowledge is Buddhist scripture. This is as unquestionable to him as empirically-verified scientific facts are to the Westerner. More than eighty percent of Myanmar's inhabitants are Buddhists, and their understanding of the universe differs profoundly from the materialistic-scientific concept. Visiting Myanmar will remain a superficial affair if you are not familiar with the fundamental ideas that have fertilized the culture you are about to meet.

There are few places left in the world where the basic cosmological idea differs so much from the Western view as they do in Myanmar. There are two reasons for this. The first reason is that the conservative Theravadin has his own answer to all the questions that Western science poses. The second is that most lay people still live in such close union with nature that the animistic heart of their Buddhist belief explains for them all those natural manifestations they do not understand. The mixture of these two elements has made Myanmar Buddhism an unassailable philosophy to the learned and a heart-warming religion for the layman, satisfying most of his emotional needs.

*The parable.* When Malunkyaputta, one of the Buddha's disciples, asked the Enlightened One about the origin of the universe, he was answered with the parable of the arrow: a man who had been hit by an arrow would not agree to have it pulled from his wound until he knew who had shot the arrow and everything about him. What

did this man look like? To which caste did he belong? Where did he live? What bow had he used and from what material was it made? However, before he could get all the answers, he died. Buddha's lesson was that it is futile for man to ask indeterminable questions. He should instead use his short life-span to work on his own salvation and to plot his course toward *nibbana*. He should strive towards the extinction of delusion, towards deliverance from all future births and thus, from suffering and misery. The question of the origin of the universe is unimportant, a mere game of empty words.

*A complex cosmology.* The universe of the Buddhist is a continuum of time, space and *kamma*. It is this latter factor that determines man's journey through an infinite number of different worlds that rise and fall in a cyclic pattern. Within them, different layers of existence correlate with the levels of insight and meditational practice which the individual has reached. This concept seems essentially Buddhist. Yet, in its physical description, it is not far from the modern physicist's vision of an ever-expanding universe. Still, even a simplified description of this 2,500-year-old theory is difficult for the Western layman to grasp.

According to Pali scriptures, the center of the world is Mount Meru, around which the sun circles. Seven concentric ranges, separated by seven broad seas, girdle the central mountain. In the outermost sea, at the cardinal points, are the four continents, each one ringed by 500 lesser islands; to the east lies Pubbavideha, to the north Uttakuru and to the west Aparagoyana. To the south is Jambudipa, home of men, the only continent where Buddhas are born, the only continent that allows *kamma* to

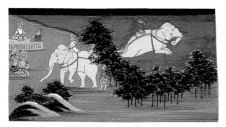

gather, and therefore the only one to offer an escape from the endless cycle of existence, the wheels of *samsara*. A Myanmar will tell you that being born as *homo sapiens* in Jambudipa, and especially in Myanmar, the country of the true faith, is the best of all possible births.

The labels are unfamiliar, but the Western mind can envision this horizontal world because it exists within the entity of time and space. Now, however, comes the difficult part: an additional, vertical stratum added to the physical one. The surface of Jambudipa is only one plane but the full gamut of human existence encompasses no fewer than 31 different levels.

*Three Worlds.* These 31 levels are structured into three clearly distinguishable realms: *Arupa Loka*, the upper realm of formlessness, *Rupa Loka*, the middle realm of fine material being and *Kama Loka*, the lower world of sensual pleasure and desire. The higher realms (also called the Brahma world) can be reached by humans only through *jhanic* meditation. The deeper the meditation and the insight, the higher the level on which one will be reborn.

*The plane of formlessness.* Arupa Loka is subdivided into four levels; it comprises the realms of infinite space, of unlimited consciousness, of nothingness, and the realm of that which is neither perception nor non-perception. However, being reborn in one of these planes does not constitute or lead to *nibbana*; it is an incorporeal existence of intellectual bliss that lasts longer than the world itself. Later, the inhabitants of this abode will be reborn in another Jambudipa where they can again begin to develop and collect enough insight and *kamma* to achieve *nibbana*.

*No taste, no smell, no touch.* The realm of Rupa Loka, the deva world, which lies beneath the sphere of formlessness, is subdivided into 16 sections. The beings who live here are free of *rupa* or desire, free of the senses of taste, smell and touch. They are not without form, but the higher the level, the finer the material they consist of. They do not need food and are born without needing parents.

To be reborn here or in *Arupa Loka*, mere good deeds are not enough: only intensive meditational practice will suffice. The 20 divisions of *Rupa* and *Arupa Loka* can only be reached by a very few. They are the ultimate aim of people who spend their life in meditation, of monks who do not have to care for their material existence but who are fed and supported by the populace (for the layman, giving to the monks is one way to gather merits). The ordinary Myanmar, the man who works in the field, who has a family and who procreates, finds himself within the realm of *Kama Loka*, dominated by sensuous desire and thought.

*Where desire reigns.* Beings in this realm have six senses, including the sense of mental impression. They live on 11 different levels that reflect their past good or evil behavior. This realm of *Kama Loka* is the real world of the Buddhist. It is here that he lives through his happiness and his sorrows. The Myanmar perceives not only the concrete physical world around him. *Kama Loka* in all of its forms, from the deep *Avici* hell to the highest abode of the gods, is real to him. All the myths of Myanmar's ancient culture have left their marks in this realm. Pre-Buddhist concepts of the world as well as animistic, Brahmanical, astrological and alchemistic ideas have found their respective niches in this cosmic structure that, despite its diverse and colorful appearance, is nevertheless a world of ethics and morals, of reward and punishment.

*Demons amongst them.* The lowest abodes of *Kama Loka* are the different hells. The punishment that awaits those reborn there is even more horrible than those described by the medieval Christian church. There are eight grades of hells – some dark, some cold, some hot, and some causing eternal pain. Just as bliss in the hea-

venly abodes lasts for an immeasurable time, so does the pain after being reborn in one of the hells. Perhaps the most wicked of all deeds that causes a person to be banished into this abyss is the wilful murder of a monk, an action so heinous that even good *kammic* deeds cannot compensate it.

Above the hells we find the animal kingdom. Rebirth as an animal is regarded as a severe punishment, even though animals live close to men, beneath, on and above the surface of Jambudipa. The *Jataka* stories, the Buddhist fables that tell about the Buddha's former lives, often depict the future Exalted One as an animal – but as an animal who could do good, collected good *kamma*, and could so move upwards to higher and more rewarding levels of existence.

The life-span of most animals is too short to allow them to perform meritorious deeds; thus, they depend on human beings to share their merits. It will take a long time for such animals to be reborn as men.

Above the kingdom of the animals is the world of *pretas*, of ghosts and specters who haunt funeral pyres and graveyards. The next level is the world of the *asuras*, or demons. They share this world with men but are seldom visible.

Next in this system of merit-bound vertical planes of existence comes the abode of man. He is the master of Jambudipa, the continent named after the mythical rose-apple tree that grows at its very end. Though life on this level is full of *dukkha*, of misery and sorrow, it nevertheless offers the only loophole to escape from the eternal wheel of *samsara*. Due to man's median position between the gods and the hells, between happiness and sorrow, he and only he is able to advance by means of his meritorious deeds.

If his meditational insight permits, he can perhaps become a "stream enterer" who will be reborn in one of the higher planes. He could even become a "non-returner," one who will be reborn in the heaven of the effortless gods, the only plane from where he finds his way directly to *nibbana*.

The inhabitants of the other three continents surrounding Mount Meru live in continuous bliss and therefore have no chance to do good. Thus, Buddhism concedes something like free will to the man of Jambudipa. This free will cannot influence man's present condition, which has been predetermined by former lives. Nevertheless, it can be directed towards his future incarnations. These he can influence by living according to the *dhamma*, the Buddha's law. This law has different implications. For the simple peasant, it is enough to follow the five basic precepts. If he doesn't kill, doesn't steal, doesn't lie, has no unlawful sexual intercourse and abstains from intoxicants, he can be sure that a similar or better life will wait for him. For *samaneras*, novices to the *sangha*, the religious order, and for *pongyis*, or monks, there are an additional 222 rules that regulate a life geared to higher wisdom and deliverance.

*Mythological beings everywhere.* Though still a part of *Kama Loka*, the six *Deva Lokas* – the abodes of the gods – come next. These include the abodes of the *Four Rulers of the Cardinal Points*, the *Thirty-three Gods*, the *Yama Gods*, the *Tusita Gods*, the *Gods of Nirmanaratis*, and the *Parinirmitavasarvatin Gods*. They are located at the foot, on the slopes, and on top of and above Mount Meru. These Buddhist gods, a remnant of pre-Buddhist Brahman cosmology, are not omnipotent beings. They are mortal, just as human beings. Their life span, consisting of continuous sensual bliss, is immensely longer than that of humans. What's more, these gods have extra physical and psychic powers. That man but seldom gets a glimpse of them is understandable. Their time continuum is so very different that a lifetime of man might be measured in minutes by the gods.

*Torn between attachment and deliverance.* Highest of all gods and the ruler of *Kama Loka* is Mara. He is the personification of sense-desire, the instigator of sensual bliss, the god of sensual love and evil, the symbol of everything the Buddha has surmounted. Man's existence is torn between the power of Mara and the law of the Buddha. The temporal satisfaction of the senses keeps man in Mara's claws, feeds him with short-lived sensations and punishes him with sorrow. Those who do not follow the path of the Buddha, those who cannot escape into *nibbana*, will always remain pawns of Mara. They will traverse *Kama Loka* between the hells and the heavens for an indeterminably long time.

The belief in such a world, in a cosmology that has changed only marginally since the fifth century before Christ, is surely not universal among modern Myanmar Buddhists. Progressives and liberals have interpreted many cosmological "facts" as only symbolic, but orthodox Theravadins still believe in the literal scriptures as the ancients did. As fundamentalists, they know that to give in, to reinterpret meanings which for millennia were based on a common understanding, would spell the end of their religion. Similar pressures in the past caused Buddhists in India to give in to the Hindu interpretation of the world and to reinterpret scriptures which until then were commonly understood. Mahayana Buddhism, as a result, underwent profound change. The orthodox Theravadin refuses to change; to him, the world interpretation of the Western physicist is just one of many cosmologies on the periphery of the *dhamma*, the True Law.

*The 37 nats.* The belief of most of the people in Myanmar, besides that which the orthodox Theravadins profess, is what is commonly called Pagoda Buddhism. Part of it is the belief in the presence and power of the 37 *nats*. Besides their animistic heritage, their story also tells the history of Myanmar since Anawrahta's time as well as any history-book. Anawrahta, the father of the Myanmar nation, selected a group of 36 animistic beings, placed their images around the terrace of the Shwezigon Pagoda in Nyaung U and announced officially that they had come under the supreme power of Thagyamin. He, the king of the *nats,* resides in the same realm as human beings, in *Kama Loka*, but on top of Mount Meru. Thagyamin is none other than Indra, also named Sakka in Pali, the Vedic god of the firmament, a disciple of Buddha. With this seemingly simple measure, Anawrahta allowed spirit worship to survive within Buddhism. Though there is no space in the fundamentalist's definition of the creed, neither for gods, nor spirits, not even for an individual soul, this arrangement satisfies perfectly the emotional needs of the common people and has thus survived into the 20th century.

Today, 15 of the 36 *nats* are not the same as the original ones that had Anawrahta's blessing, and represent heroes identifiable from the later history of the country. The other 21 all seem to be more or less mythological figures from the pre-Bagan era.

Today, Myanmar's state schools teach Newton's Law. State schools are gradually replacing the *pongyi kyaung*, the old monastery school, once prevalent in Central Myanmar. Still, it will take a long time, and it will need many changes in the daily life of the people, before a purely physical interpretation of the cosmos can supplant this kaleidoscopic landscape of the mind. For the Myanmars, the complex unity of *Kama Loka*, where the *kammic* power of man is one of the structural elements of the universe, is much more attractive and sensible than anything modern science has to offer.

*The plain of Bagan.*

*A kyaung, a dwelling place for monks.*

This realm of Bagan is so named
because it is the fairest and dearest of lands.
It is called Arimaddana
because its people are warriors
who vanquish their foes,
and even its name is terrible.
Its folk are free from pain and danger,
they are skilled in every art,
they possess the tools of every craft,
they are wealthy,
the revenues are past telling
and the land is full of useful things.

Verily it is a land more to be desired
than Himavanta, the fairy land.
It is a glorious realm
and its people are famed
for their splendor and power.

*Tun Nyein, Inscriptions of Bagan,*
*Pinya and Ava Monastery.*
*Inscription 1343 AD.*

*A paddle-wheel steamer on the Ayeyarwady in 1855.*

*A painter's view of the ruined city.*

# ARIMADDANA

*The Dawn of a Nation*

**S**hortly after the historic day in 1044 AD when Anawrahta's mythical spear, Areindama, pierced the body of his half-brother Sokkate, making Anawrahta king over the 19 villages in the plain of Bagan, a yellow-clad recluse by the name of Shin Arahan was brought into the new ruler's presence. This Buddhist monk, son of an Indian Brahman in Thaton, turned Anawrahta's mind toward a religion that was breathing its last in India, where it was being routed by the steady and merciless advance of Islam.

*A nation builder at work.* Bagan, until then a relatively unimportant walled city on the bank of the Ayeyarwady in Central Myanmar, which was then known as *Arimaddana,* the City of the Enemy Crusher, entered history as the cradle of a religious reformation whose impact is still felt today.

Anawrahta was what modern political scientists would call a nation builder, one of those rare, true masters of the art of statesmanship. He knew that if he wanted to reign over more than just a few villages as his forefathers had done, he had to become the promoter of a unifying belief and the protector of a common ideal that would tie people together. Up until that time, religion had been characterized by spirit worship mixed with the degenerated Buddhism of the Ari monks, the Naga cult and elements of Brahmanistic idolatry. The era was ripe for change.

*The mighty Dhammayangyi.*

The "11 villages of Kyaukse" were Anawrahta's economic mainstay. Though situated in the dry plain of Upper Myanmar, they were watered by four ancient rivers and a system of artificial irrigation that had been in use since time immemorial. This plain of Kyaukse provided enough surplus paddy to feed not only the royal household but also artisans, monks and soldiers, without whom Bagan would never have grown beyond its original tribal structure.

Shin Arahan, the pious hermit monk (whose original sculpted features can still be seen in Bagan's Ananda Temple), introduced Anawrahta to the conservative interpretation of a philosophy that during its more than 1,500 years of existence, had been proven to engender sense and commitment in the hearts of its followers. Myanmar's history had reached a turning point: Buddhism provided the long-sought ethic fabric which was needed to create a superior culture, and marked the Bagan Era as one of humanity's most brilliant periods.

*A Universal Monarch.* Anawrahta had his own personal challenge. The ideal he wanted to live up to was that of the Mauryan King Ashoka, the 3rd century BC Indian ruler who was an outstanding example of a Buddhist *cakkavatti,* a "Universal Monarch." It was Anawrahta's aim to become just such a "Universal Monarch." He strove to become the benevolent ruler who as *dhammaraja* was defender of the law, as *sangharaja* was protector of the church, and as *kammaraja* built temples and stupas to share merit with his people. Anawrahta concentrated his wisdom and his ability toward achieving no less than that.

*Religion as the driving force.* Shin Arahan's supplication for a set of the *Tipitaka* (*Tripitaka* in Sanskrit) scriptures prompted Anawrahta to turn to war. He fought the Mon empire in southern Myanmar and returned with 30 elephant-loads of palm-leaf scriptures. While the chronicles mention the *Tipitaka* scriptures, modern researchers doubt that he ever received them; instead of this, they say, he brought back copies of the *Jatakas.*

The *Jatakas*, today seen as the most ancient set of morality stories that later found their way through the Middle East to become the basic stock of European fables, hark back to an era even before the time when Buddha was born. These stories have

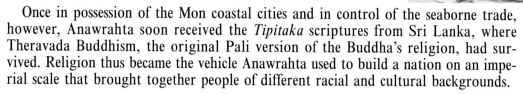

*Temples on the Ayeyarwady's shore.*

been handed down orally from generation to generation of illiterate peasants.

Once in possession of the Mon coastal cities and in control of the seaborne trade, however, Anawrahta soon received the *Tipitaka* scriptures from Sri Lanka, where Theravada Buddhism, the original Pali version of the Buddha's religion, had survived. Religion thus became the vehicle Anawrahta used to build a nation on an imperial scale that brought together people of different racial and cultural backgrounds.

*A glorious era.* In the more than 900 years since Anawrahta's reign, Buddhism has been the unifying theme enabling Myanmar to survive centuries of war and migration. The first centuries of this millennium, the years during which Bagan flourished, were also the crowning years for other Southeast Asian kingdoms. In the Indonesian archipelago, Srivijaya, a wealthy Indianized state, held a virtual trade monopoly on all goods that passed from the East to Arabia. In the Khmer empire, Suryavarman II, a contemporary of Myanmar's king Kyanzittha, oversaw the building of Angkor Vat, Southeast Asia's greatest single religious monument. This was the time when the seed of Indian culture, planted in foreign soil, came into full bloom. Vaishnavism, Shaivism and Mahayana Buddhism sometimes blended and produced the timeless beauty of Southeast Asia's religious sculpture and architecture.

*An Indian heritage.* In Myanmar, these Indian craftsmen — whose handwriting can also be traced at the Borobudur, at Angkor Vat and Angkor Thom — came in whole guilds. Some were refugees from the advancing Islamic forces; others came as regular contracted workers to help build the temples of Bagan.

The inhabitants of Myanmar's Rakhine and Ramanadesa coasts already had long-standing relations with the Indian subcontinent. Traders and Brahman priests had settled at the river mouths in the first centuries AD and it was through them that Theravada Buddhism established its first foothold on the mainland of Southeast Asia.

Further north, the earliest influence came from Sanskrit Buddhism, from the Mahayana and Tantra variants of this world-shaking creed. These, however, were not as firmly embedded in the hearts of the people and lacked the rigorous adherence to scriptural order which was found in the Theravada.

By the time Anawrahta came to power, religious decadence had set in. It is no wonder, therefore, that Manuha, the captured Thaton King, saw the Bamars (the Burmans) as merely a barbaric tribe from the northern wastelands without any valuable culture. All this changed within a generation as Mon scripture, Mon architecture and the more cosmopolitan lifestyle of the coastal people took root at Bagan. The conquered thus became the teachers, largely because Anawrahta had 30,000 Mons — artisans, monks and traders — transferred to the capital of his once landlocked kingdom.

*A line of great kings.* However, it took more than just one charismatic leader to stabilize what was to become a multiracial nation. History endowed Myanmar with two more kings within a century whose deeds fit the description of a "Universal Monarch": Kyanzittha and his grandson Alaungsithu. Together with Anawrahta, they were the founding fathers of a Buddhist nation the equal of Ashoka's legendary kingdom. For 250 years, this nation of Arimaddana paraded its greatness.

*Meritorious deeds.* There were once 13,000 temples, stupas and other religious structures in Bagan. Though today only 2,260 remain, these monuments have been a lasting inspiration to the Myanmar people over the centuries. They serve not only as reminders of the *dhamma*, the timeless Buddhist law; they also tell of a bygone glory, one that established a cultural continuity which endured the Mongol, Shan, Chinese, British and Japanese invasions of the country.

27

*The Gawdawpalin Temple.*

*The ruined bell-columns of Kyanzittha's palace.*

Inscriptions that have survived nine centuries of heat and rain tell us that the aim of life during Bagan's epoch of brilliance was not one of personal enrichment. The law of *kamma*, which led men to earn merit by endowments and donations, was the driving ethic. An air of constant striving for goodness lay over the era. Although the king was virtually the master of all his subjects' life and death, he was no god-king and was himself bound to the *dhamma*. He depended on his advisers and on acceptance by the *sangha*, the fraternity of the monks. Oriental despotism, as 19th-century European scholars called this system of government, took on a very different aspect under a benevolent ruler. In times of chaos, the ruler offered the only possible way to amass men and material to fight against enemies and natural forces.

For the Bagan kings, the enemy was mainly an eternal one: man's bondage to his *kamma*. The weapon to free his subjects was the *dhamma*, meritorious deeds on a scale previously unknown in history. The reason for building the temples and stupas was not only to propagate a reformed faith to an illiterate populace; it was the merit to be earned and shared that motivated the Buddhist court to build on such a grandiose scale.

*Temple slaves.* Bagan was hierarchically structured, and as with today's castes in India, people lived in quarters defined by their occupations; the court settled within the walled city and the artisans, farmers and servants beyond the city walls. Members of one of these castes, the *paya kywan*, the pagoda or temple slaves, were bonded by heredity to certain endowments. They and their offspring were to be the keepers of the temples and the images within. The income from glebe lands (land donated to monks) and whole villages was often part of these bequests.

Under the circumstances that governed life in the era of the temple builders, being a pagoda slave was often preferable to serving the crown directly since the life of a single human being didn't have much value and everybody was at the instant disposal of the king. Only in 1947 was the status of the *paya kywan* officially and formally abolished. For many, however, this abolition was totally meaningless, since everyone knew about the ancient curse that befalls those who do not live up to their inherited obligations, including those who were instrumental in abolishing this ancient kind of slavery. *Avici* hell, the deepest of all hells, awaits them. Buddhaghosa, still today seen as the greatest authority on Buddhist law, wrote in the 5th century:

*"Although anyone shall give a substitute for a pagoda slave, he cannot liberate him, for the slaves set aside by kings as consecrated property for the 5,000 years of the church are fixed and settled for these 5,000 years. Whoever from king downward shall break the continuity of the consecrated and resumes the property, shall pass into the lowest hell. Slaves who have been offered to pagodas can only be employed in cleaning pagodas. They must not wait on kings or anyone else. If those who have great power employ pagoda slaves, they will lose their power and die a frightful death; they will come to misery and destruction."*

Some of the pious local visitors you see offering food and flowers and doing the ritual washing of the images today, might be descendants of original Bagan *paya kywan*. In Bagan and Myinkaba, these families might also still hold the keys to some of the temples that are closed to the public.

Far from the royal court, the simple peasant and the monk in his monastery in remote villages lived lives that were already democratic in character. Elders and elected representatives of village councils, together with the egalitarian nature of the *sangha*, or fraternity of the monks, provided counterbalance

*Thiripiytsaya village is built on historic ground.*

to an otherwise often oppressive era. Chronicles report the grave wrongdoings of certain rulers; but at the same time they also tell how these men came to an inglorious end. Many kings, however, not only promoted Buddhism but even conducted their personal lives as examples for the faithful. For example, Alaungsithu once said:

*"May I always be conscious and aware*
*Of kindness done to me!*
*Union of ill friends be far from me!*
*Beholding the distress of men and*
*Deathless gods.*
*I would put forth mine energies*
*And save men, spirits, gods,*
*From seas of endless change!"*

For a king to express such feelings is not common in human history. But during that era, in Myanmar, Alaungsithu was not alone. Other rulers also left inscriptions that demonstrate their yearning for *nibbana* and their profound belief in a world where gods, *nats*, men and ghosts lived together – but where only men could earn merit and share it with the other beings of the universe.

*Bagan is grandiose.* There is no other ancient temple city so large and so well preserved in the world. The absence of secular buildings in Bagan tells a lot about the attitudes of its people during its heyday. The king's palace was built of wood, whereas the temples were built to survive until the coming of the next Buddha. According to the scriptures, Gautama's reign lasts 5,000 years; when Bagan was actually built, more than 1,500 of these years had already past. Some of the temples seem sturdy enough to survive the 2,500 years that are still to come.

*Everything crumbles, the word survives.* This is the message Myanmar has written all over the remainder of its ancient culture: while everything crumbles, decays and is subject to the law of *samsara*, the word of the Buddha survives. Here is the origin not only of the nation but also of the unique Myanmar brand of Buddhism. When Anawrahta laid the foundation for this happy syncretism, this reconciliation of animistic and Buddhist beliefs, no one could have expected this to be the unaltered, living religion of the nation nearly a thousand sand years later. The stalwart reminders of the *dhamma* in Bagan, together with the images of the 37 *nats* that are still enshrined in a shed behind the Shwezigon Pagoda, have shaped the mind of the Myanmars. Even in the remotest hamlet, people are aware of Bagan's time-honored beauty and its awe-inspiring eminence. If there is one image that has formed the Myanmar nation and given it a common heritage, it is Bagan.

*Fetching water from the river.*

**W**hen the temples of Bagan were built,
the light of the *dhamma* rose over the country.

**R**eligious structures, 2,260 in number, all built
to improve *kamma* and gain merit, are strewn without
apparent design all over the plain of Bagan.

**T**oday, as during the heyday of Bagan, the weather-beaten
Bamar peasant is the indestructible backbone of the nation.

**T**he mighty Dhammayangyi has nothing of the sublimity
of the Anada, upon which it was based, but it shows
the finest masonry on the plain of Pagan.

38

**F**or 800 years Myanmars have bowed for protection
and blessing under the bended arms of the Ananda Buddha.

Unlike the lofty halls of contemporaneous
Gothic cathedrals, the interiors of Mon-style temples
are like caves; narrow, cool and dim: ideal places
for meditation.

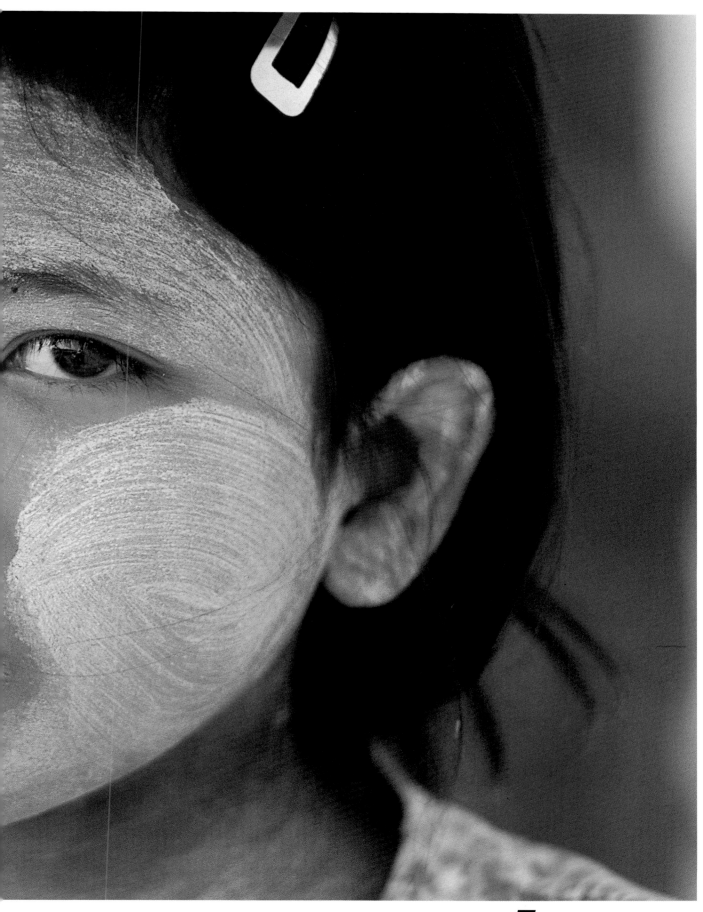

*T*hanaka bark powder is the
universal cosmetic for Myanmar women.

“ . . . their getting aged, becoming toothless, gray haired
and wrinkled, the failing of their vital forces,
the wearing out of their senses: this is called decay. ”
*Abidhamma Pitaka*

**T**he social function of the *pongyi* is to transmit
the Buddhist way of life from generation to generation,
irrespective of political trends.

**T**he light of the *dhamma* continues to illuminate
the isolated country on the banks of the Ayeyarwady,
even as it loses its grip in the surrounding countries.

*The hub of the Myanmar Empire, circa 1855.*

*A nat and a princess.*

*A princess and her maid.*

*A prince and his servant.*

The Blessed One turned the boy not back.
And the people with the Blessed One
were not able to stop him.
And so he went with the Blessed One
even up to the grove.
And the Blessed One thought:
"This wealth, this property of his father's
which he is asking for,
perishes in the using,
and brings vexation with it!
I will give him the sevenfold Ariyan wealth
which I obtained under the Bo-tree,
and make him the heir of a spiritual inheritance!"
And he said to Sariputta:
"Well then do thou, Sariputta,
receive Rahula into the Order."

*The Buddha takes his son into the Order.*
*The story of the lineage.*

**A**t some time before the 9th century AD, an uncivilized tribe emerged from the gorges of the southbound Himalayan rivers, somewhere to the north of today's Mandalay. As they stood at the fringe of the hills, dressed in not much more than simple loincloths and tattoos, with the torrid plain of Upper Myanmar and the malaria-infested estuary of the broad river ahead of them, one of humanity's longest migrations was about to come to an end.

For nearly 2,000 years, these tribesmen had migrated from Gansu in northwestern China. They passed the source of the Yellow River in northeastern Tibet, then settled temporarily in Yunnan before moving on over the mountains of northeast Myanmar and down into the rice-growing plain that is continually watered by the Ayeyarwady on its way to the Andaman Sea.

*A long march to nationhood.* Chinese records from the second millennium BC tell of the Ch'iang, a race of shepherds and goatherds who inhabited the loess (clay and silt) plateau to the west of the Han Chinese homeland. They were the ancestors of the modern Bamars (Burmans). Their culture at that time seems to have been as developed as that of the Chinese: they already used bronze vessels and tools. The pattern of their painted pottery can still be traced on modern Myanmar earthenware. But sheep transform meadows into wasteland where cattle cannot graze and the Chinese expansionists, who outnumbered the Ch'iang and who were slowly moving westwards, were cattle breeders. The Ch'iang's lifestyle was not easily adaptable; they had to choose between submission to their new masters or moving away from their homeland. In the end they opted for the latter, without knowing what hardship it would bring to future generations until the day when a new homeland was found.

During their 2,000-year migration, the Ch'iang lost most of their ancient cultural traits. They had to trek over mountains, through deserts and jungles; they became nomads, jungle dwellers and hill people. Much of their original Neolithic culture was replaced with more practical techniques of survival. They learned to hunt, to fight and to breed horses and became experts with the bow and arrow. Perhaps most important of all, they developed some immunity to tropical fevers and sores. The moment when they stood at the edge of the mountains, about to descend into the blistering heat of the lowlands, one could have called them barbarians, with some justification. Therefore, it is astonishing to find these people at the core of Southeast Asian history within only a few centuries of their first contact with the Indianized culture of the coast.

In the Ayeyarwady valley, the new arrivals found a land already irrigated by the Mon, a race that had entered the country 1,000 years earlier through the valley of the Thanlwin (Salween), and their racial brethren, the Pyu. Here on the Kyaukse Plain, four rivers – the Samon, Panlaung, Zawgyi and Myitnge – provided a year-round water supply to the flat land beneath the Shan mountains. In this fertile basin, the Bamars established their first settlements not far from the ruined capitals of the Pyus with whom they mingled during subsequent generations. Here, they also built their own capitals.

The first was Bagan, followed by Sagaing, Innwa (Ava), Amarapura and Mandalay. History has proved the wisdom of their choice. From the sites of their respective capitals, the royal courts were able to control the economy by administering the irrigation of the land and the main waterways.

*Mindon Min, the founder of Mandalay.*

*A prince at the Mandalay court.*

*Water, rice and royalty.* If you travel today by boat from Bagan up the Ayeyarwady, passing the mighty confluence with the Chindwinn and then turning towards the east, you can still see the remnants of ancient power centers strung along the river banks like pearls on a string. Sagaing, with its myriad temples, pagodas and monasteries, stretches along the northern embankment where the only bridge spans the Ayeyarwady. Directly opposite, on an artificial island at the mouth of the Myitnge River, the ruins of Innwa (Ava) mark the site of the city from which the Bamars controlled the country for the longest period of time.

The 12.5 miles (20 km) from Innwa to Mandalay are dotted with religious and royal ruins, most of which date from the last dynasty (1752–1885) when the Myanmar kings resided here. This short stretch of the Ayeyarwady can be thought of as the nation's heartland. Here, the Bamars had their base; here, they tackled the Shan, thus deciding who would finally dominate the land; here, after defeating the Mon in the 18th century, the renewal of Myanmar hegemony began. However, this ascendancy lasted only for a few decades, because once they reached the border with British India, after annexing Manipur, the Myanmars found themselves confronted by European weapons and the colonial thirst for expansion.

In 1852, after the Second Anglo-Burmese War, the British occupied all of Lower Myanmar. The Kingdom of Ava (Innwa), as Myanmar was then known, became a landlocked state. This dependence made it easy prey for the final invasion by the British. The revolutionary ideas, both Islamic and Western, that had swept through other parts of Southeast Asia in preceding centuries had little effect upon Innwa, where the court had an ostentatious lifestyle only marginally different from that of Kyanzittha's court in the 12th century.

The kings of the Konbaung Dynasty (1752–1885) often used to shift their capitals to different locations after coming to power. When King Mindon ascended the throne after replacing his insane brother Pagan, he founded Mandalay, 7 miles (12 km) to the northeast of the then-capital Amarapura. But no matter where its capital was located, the Myanmar government was still called "The Court of Ava."

*The Center of the Universe.* Visiting Mandalay today, you can still recognize how exotic this city must have been 120 years ago. Though only the walls have survived the ravages of time, the government's archaeological department is cautiously remodeling the wooden palace buildings, and soon, the splendor of a bygone era will be vividly recreated. There is something, however, that will not be visible any more, something that needs the full power of one's imagination: the human element of a bygone era that made the palace the focal point of power. The pomp is missing, as are the intrigues and servility that marked an autocratic time.

For the people living under its influence, the Lion Throne of Mandalay was really the "Center of the Universe." This description is quite appropriate considering that it was here that the interface between the human world and the worlds beyond was to be found. To arouse the king's temporary indignation was more often than not ample reason to be put to death. Though human, the king himself was unassailable by the rest of the population. To be born into such a high position, he must have gathered an immense amount of merit in his former lives. Thus, even a brutal and cruel king seemed closer to Buddhahood than a pious *sayadaw*. It is this Buddhist tenet that, even today, makes it difficult to instill Theravada Buddhists with a genuine understanding of democratic rules. The king was required to have eight queens (not counting the minor ones), of which the Southern Queen was the Chief Queen; she had to be a half-sister of the king. And there were plenty of half-sisters and brothers. Mindon had 45 queens and some 70 surviving children. Most of them were cruelly assassi-

*Thibaw and his Queen Supayalat.*

nated in February 1879 when, after Mindon's death, Thibaw, one of his later sons, was swept to power. In those days, the palace was teeming with servants and courtiers. For the king alone there were 35 pages, 40 tea servers, 60 betel-box bearers, 100 slipper bearers, 40 bearers of the White Umbrellas, 10 lectors who read from the sacred scriptures, 15 messengers, 450 armed guards, 220 bearers of the Royal Swords, and 155 chamberlains who had to be on duty within the palace walls. In addition, there were innumerable servants waiting on the rest of the royal family, which consisted frequently of more than a hundred heads.

*A symbol of Buddhist faith.* Mandalay was built using archaic Brahmanist symbols and maxims, ancient Chinese architectural patterns and the ideas of the Buddhist faith chiseled in stone. When Mindon had this city built during the 1850s he had to follow the Brahmin *ponnas'* and astrologers' advice: consequently, 52 persons are said to be buried alive under the corners and gates of the walls and the palace. These guardian spirits, however, didn't do much to preserve the monarchy nor the city itself. Despite this, the palaces were still standing deep into this century.

On 20 March 1945, British troops, engaging Japanese troops in Mandalay, shelled the "Golden City." The wooden structures caught fire and burned to the ground, possibly due to the shelling or possibly because the palace was incinerated by the fleeing Japanese. The "Cluster of Gems," the "Center of the Universe," a unique regal city built entirely on an ancient, oriental pattern, had ceased to exist.

Mindon, the regal city's creator, was more modern in outlook than his predecessors. He tried to create a sense of national unity by ceaselessly propagating ancient Buddhist ideals. The Fifth Buddhist Synod, which Mindon convened in this city, symbolized the king's intention to make Mandalay the "Center of the Universe" and – following the Buddha's personal prophecy – the "New Jerusalem" of the Buddhist faith and Myanmar renewal.

*The Fifth Buddhist Synod.* In the past, the architectural layout of Buddhist structures had been used to educate the lay people, but Mindon's idea of spreading the faith was more modern. Since Buddhist scriptures were traditionally written on palm-leaves which would decay, Mindon had the complete Buddhist Canon chiseled onto 729 marble slabs, each of which was then covered by a small pagoda. The Kuthodaw Pagoda, at the base of Mandalay Hill, has been called "The World's Largest Book" ever since. In its vicinity, around the Sandamuni Pagoda, are a further 1,774 stone tablets that contain the commentaries on the *Tipitaka* Canon. Mindon's reign was one of a truly Buddhist monarch and, by convening the Fifth Buddhist Synod in 1871–72, he made Mandalay a center of this creed.

The reign of his son Thibaw was quite different. The cruelty he inflicted on his brothers when he ascended the throne may have been common in medieval times, but in 1878, with the telegraph connecting Mandalay with the rest of the world and steamships regularly plying the Ayeyarwady, such behavior was certainly inappropriate. The British, having already occupied the southern part of the country, were only waiting for a good reason to subdue a kingdom that seemed unable to catch up with modern times. In the year 1885, after a minor dispute between a timber company and the Myanmar government, the British came up the Ayeyarwady and, against only minimal resistance, occupied the new capital. They sent King Thibaw and his queen Supayalat into exile in India, where they vanished from the pages of history. With them disappeared the last example of a genuine medieval Buddhist kingdom.

*Marginal Western influence.* For a decade, the British had to fight local guerrillas, who even without central coordination made the hill tracts and villages of Upper Myanmar ungovernable for the viceroy's administration. As it had done time and again when the country was in a period of decline, Upper Myanmar produced the men and ideas to secure the continuity of the indigenous Myanmar culture. Western technology and weapons had demonstrated their unquestionable superiority, so these alien influences were incorporated into that unique mixture that became modern Myanmar culture.

*Fables and spirits.* Still, many of the old traditions remain. Off the main tourist routes, the belief in spirits is an important part of life. Numerous indicators of archaic influences are abundantly visible, be it the *nat*-Festival at Taungbyon, some 18 miles (32 km) from Mandalay, where every August a multitude of people meet to worship two of the 37 national *nats*; or the palmists, astrologers, soothsayers and tattooers who populate the stairways of Mandalay Hill.

What you see on the hill is neither Buddhist nor Western scientific; these are animistic remnants of a past which has been preserved in much greater depth than meets the eye. In places where people have lived unchanged lives since time immemorial, with the monsoon sweeping regularly over them and the fruits of their labor ripening season after season in their fields, there is a different conception of reality than in the midst of fast-living city dwellers. Since they are cut off from mainstream developments beyond their finite world, it is the people's belief in the spirits inhabiting their environment that explains the unexplainable in their daily lives. They depend on an environment that is populated by forces of good and evil to counterbalance their own psyche.

The tradition is an ancient one: the *Jatakas*, the fables that describe Buddha's 547 former lives in the incarnation of various different animals, have been the bible of illiterate Buddhist peasants through more than two millennia. In essence, they contain the basic ethic and moral precepts of humankind and were handed on by word of mouth from generation to generation.

*The mystical shin-pyu valley.* Also recognizable wherever Buddhism has its strongholds in the contemporary Myanmar landscape is the profound Indian heritage. One such place is Sagaing, the former

*A "White Elephant", one of the signs of a "Universal Ruler," in front of the Mandalay Palace.*

capital which today is a village of 600 monasteries and 5,000 monks not far from Mandalay. It is Myanmar's foremost retreat for persons who want to renounce the world, and for those seeking a quiet place to meditate. Sagaing is also the place to which families of standing in Central Myanmar send their sons to be accepted into the *sangha*, to follow the path of Buddha and his son Rahula. Here, the boys undergo their *shin-pyu*, their initiation ceremony, the first decisive step in a man's quest of *nibbana*.

As long as this ceremony continues to be performed on nearly every Myanmar boy, it is very unlikely that the old Myanmar values will vanish. Every young man who starts his adult life with weeks of meditation in the hills of Sagaing will be imbued with the incomparable beauty inherent in the traditional Myanmar way of life.

*A lady of the palace.*

55

**T**he temple-dotted hills of Sagaing are
sacred ground for Myanmar Buddhists.

It is hard to turn away from the Enlightened One
at the U Min Thonze Pagoda.

59

**H**ereditary slaves, *paya kywans*, were dedicated
to the temples. Their descendants still do the job voluntarily.
Their *kamma* is at stake.

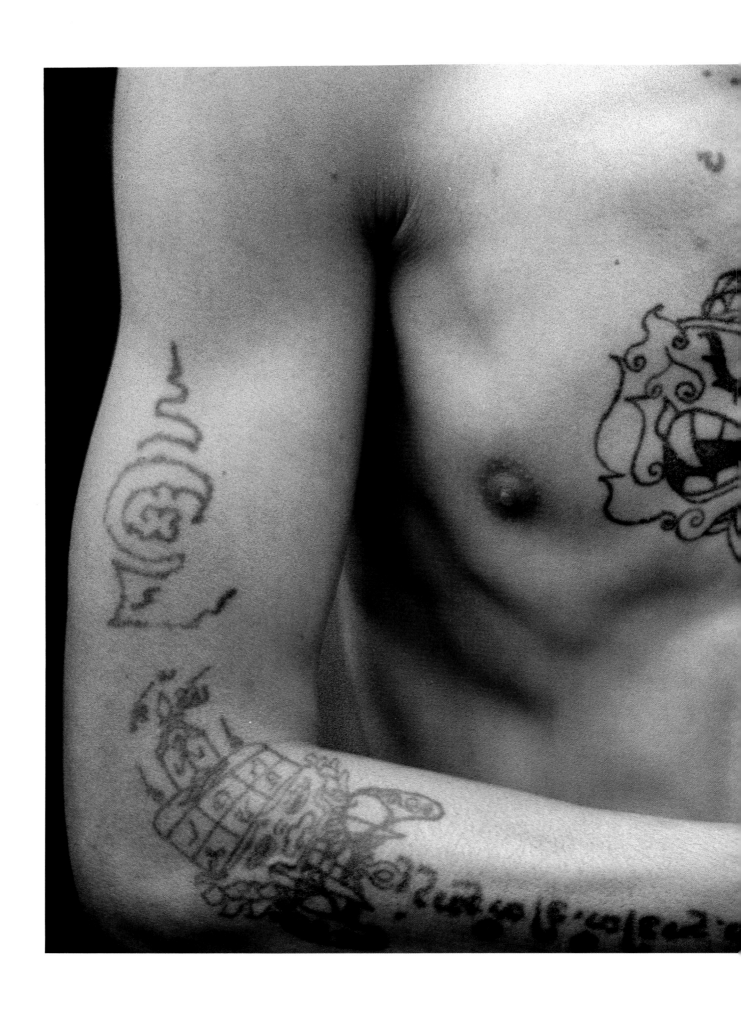

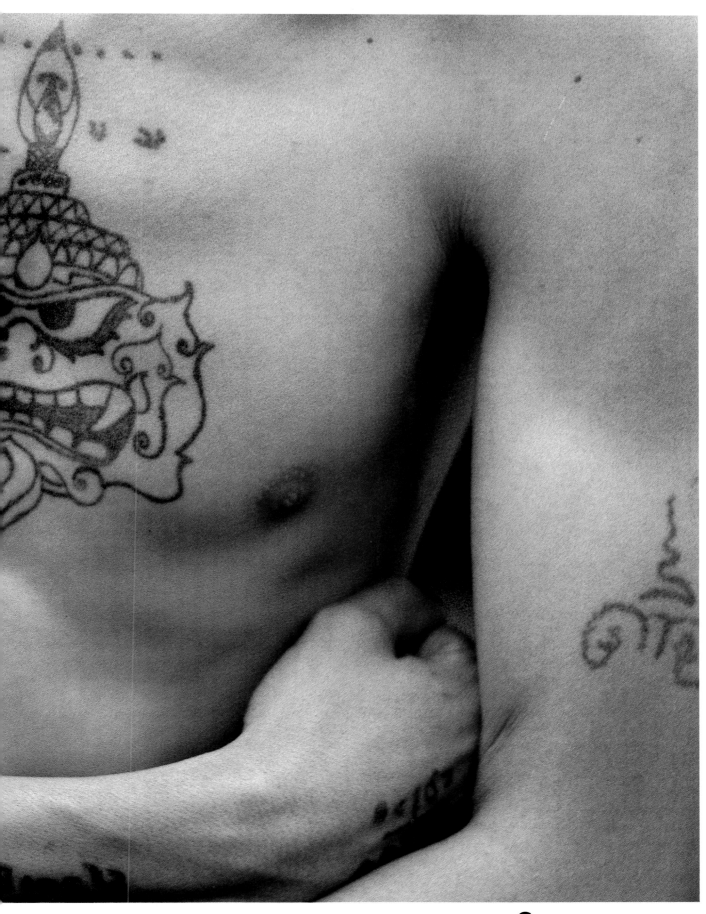

Some Myanmars still believe that tatoos shield them from evil influences and make them invulnerable.

*N*ats: They might be spirits, dwellers of a
heavenly realm, or actual historical figures.

63

The matchless Maha Muni, once venerated
as the palladium of independent Rakhine,
is thought to be as old as the Buddhist faith itself.

65

*T*ongas, horse-drawn carriages, are still
the principal means of transport in Mandalay.

67

**D**uring the evening hours, when the dust
of the dry Upper Myanmar plain slowly settles,
all colors change to gold.

**P**roviding food for the monks enhances one's *kamma*.
It's the donor who has to give thanks for the opportunity
he is given to collect merit.

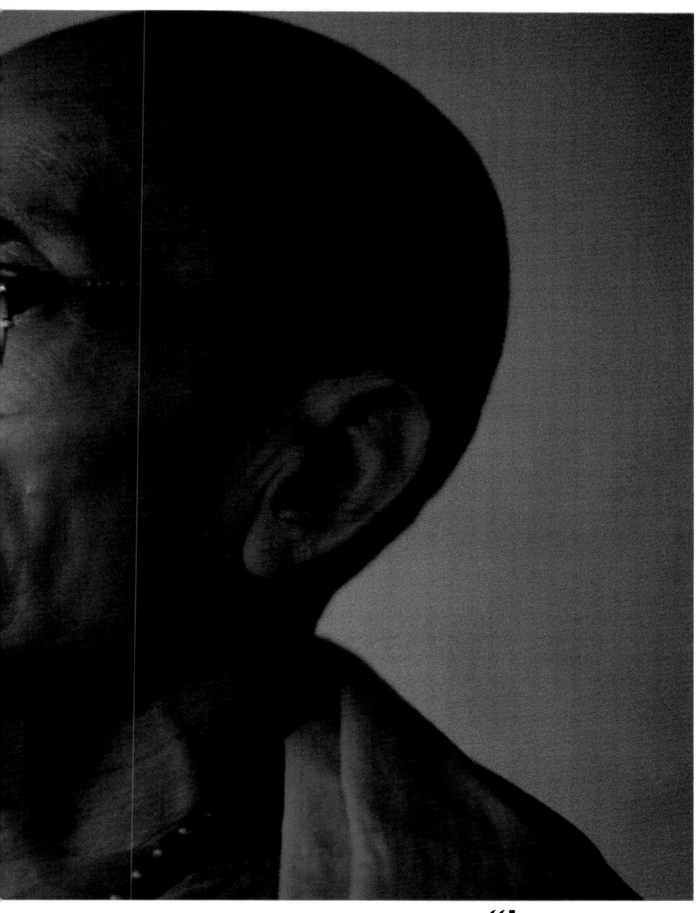

**"I**n him, *bikkhus*, who has calmness of the mind, the restlessness-and-worry that has not arisen does not arise, the restlessness-and-worry that has already arisen is abandoned.**"**
*Ninth Sutta, Anguttara Nikaya*

72

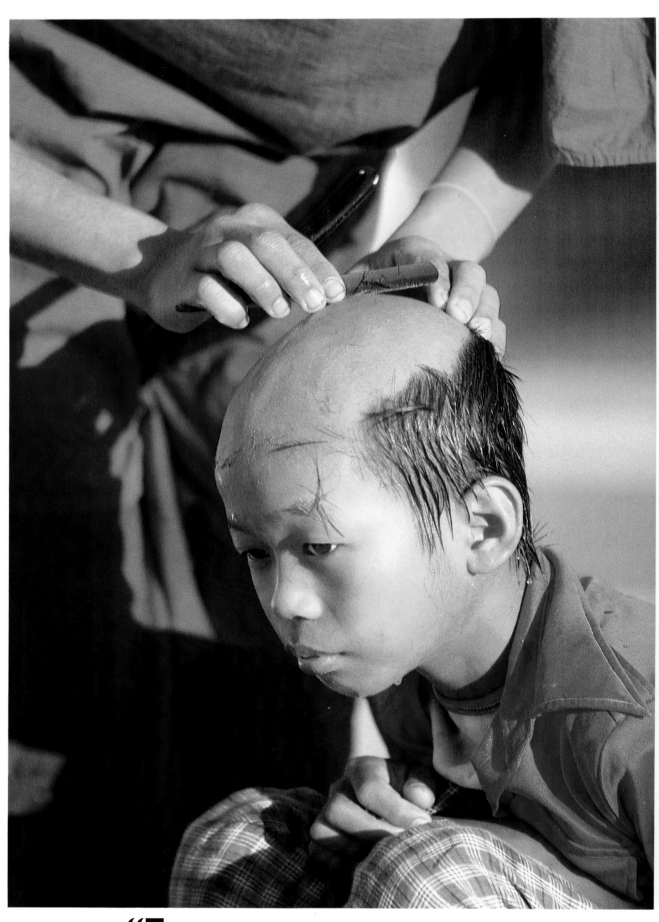

**"T**hese are mere filth as regards color, shape, smell
and location. These are not I, not mine, not a soul or a being,
but are impermanent, a cause of suffering and not self.**"**
*Samyutta Nikaya*

**A** young *samanera* is the pride of his family.

**"T**he three robes and the alms bowl, razor,
needle and girdle, and a water strainer:
these eight are the wealth of the monk devout.**"**

*The Story of the Lineage*

"**R**everend Sir, I ask for initiation in order to enable me
to escape from the trouble of *samsara*.
For the second time, reverend Sir, I ask for initiation.
For the third time, reverend Sir, I ask for initiation."
*Buddhist initiation formula*

**"R**everend Sir, may you be pleased to give me
the robe and, out of compassion for me, may you initiate
me as a novice so that I may be able to overcome all
the suffering in the round of rebirths and attain *nibbana*.**"**
*Buddhist initiation formula*

**T**he first step on the way to overcome
the eternal suffering of *samsara* is done.

*The visit of a suitor.*

*A tea ceremony.*

*A family meal.*

*A sayadaw, a venerated monk.*

**W**hen they were all assembled, the Lord Omniscient
thus addressed the image of himself:
"I shall pass into Nibbana in my eightieth year,"
he said,
"but you, instinct with my essence,
will live the five thousand years
which I have prescribed for the duration of the Religion."

*The Maha Muni prophecy, Sappadanapakarana.*

**M**yanmar is divided into three distinctly different zones that also serve as ethnic watersheds. The mountain ranges in the east, running south from the mighty Himalayas to the Isthmus of Kra, are the home of mostly non-Bamar hill tribes. The Ayeyarwady river basin and the alluvial plain in Myanmar's center are largely peopled by the Bamars themselves. And finally, clearly divided from the rest of the country by the hills of the Rakhine Yoma to the west, is the fertile coastal strip of Rakhine (Arakan).

Until a short while ago there was only scant interest in the people of this region. The plight of the Rohingyas, who recently made headlines when fleeing to Bangladesh, temporarily drew the attention of the world to this coastal state.

For too long has it been cut off from the rest of the world. For the government in Yangon it was always "beyond the hills," politically unstable, religiously divided, and in its racial composition, far from pure-blooded. Foreigners were kept out.

Rakhine is today a state within the Union of Myanmar. Compared with the region inhabited by the Bamars themselves, it is a backyard of the country. But that wasn't always so; there were times when powerful and haughty kings reigned here independently. The remains of their once splendid capital cities are now buried under unkempt vegetation. Along the Kaladan and the Lemro Rivers you can still find a multitude of disintegrating, ancient structures that bear witness to a great past. Thus, Rakhine itself is a constant reminder of the Buddhist notion that everything is in a state of flux and nothing, not even the mightiest kingdom, is permanent.

*Crumbling idols.* For those who are granted permission, traveling to Rakhine can be a once-in-a-lifetime experience. There is no such thing as a tourist infrastructure here, nor are there other amenities to which Western travelers are accustomed, but there is an atmosphere of mystery, a people who play out their lives as paddy-farmers in a way that has remained unchanged for centuries, and a cultural diversity that is rarely encountered elsewhere.

It is inland, on the banks of Rakhine's great rivers, where one finds the remnants of ancient civilizations. Like the Greek and Roman ruins along the shores of the Mediterranean, so too the disintegrating images, stupas and temples in this region tell the story of vanished kingdoms that flourished here during the first millennium AD. Ruins of ancient settlements, more often than not covered by the encroaching tropical vegetation, are bound to contain spectacular archaeological finds.

As in so many other regions of Myanmar, it is the work of the imagination, fueled by the fragrance and the fairy-tale views, that makes this part of the country so otherworldly. Fantastic pictures of the past can be recreated by descriptions of people like the Augustinian Friar Manrique, who lived in Mrauk-U in the 1630s. Manrique was there at a time when the Mogul Empire was near its zenith, when Islam clashed with Buddhism and when the Portuguese tried to impose themselves, through their superior weapons, upon a people who had found their strengths in runic science, alchemy and Brahman rituals.

Today, the people who live on the offshore islands here and along the eastern coast of the Bay of Bengal are of a peculiar mixture. Undoubtedly of Mongoloid extraction, they have so much Indian blood in their veins that their very features bear witness to the land's turbulent history – a past that reflects Rakhine's vulnerable location between antagonistic races and religions. In times long past, this was a Hindu land. The first immigrants came from Bengal and Bihar in India during a time of Brahman resurgence. This was a time in which the old Vedic religion was reinstated in its new Hindu guise. Buddhism, which had spread over most of India in the centu-

*Poling the boat upriver.*

ries before Christ, survived in its Mahayana form; however, it was often indistinguishable from Hinduism.

*Homeland of the "Great Sage."* Chronicles, whose reliability is often questioned, record a line of kings reaching back to the year 2666 BC. The sources that tell of the kingdom of Dhannavati which flourished here at the beginning of the Christian era are better founded. The image of the sacred Maha Muni, the guardian of Rakhine's independence, was created in this bygone realm, and it was still standing as late as 1784.

Legend tells us that the Maha Muni image of the Buddha is as old as the faith itself. Certainly, it made north Rakhine a Holy Land for the Buddhists. Pilgrims from all over South and Southeast Asia flocked to the old site of Dhannavati. They came to worship an image for which, it was said, the Omniscient One himself stood as model. Dhannavati was succeeded by Vesali, a kingdom that drew its name from the legendary Licchavi city in India. This last of the ancient Rakhine kingdoms vanished during the invasion by Mongolian tribes in 957 AD.

*The arrival of the Tibeto-Burmans.* All of a sudden, Rakhine changed. The invading tribes made the country face east, away from India. As ancient Myanmar began to flex its muscles, the profound changes initiated by Bagan also transformed Rakhine. The Tibeto-Burmans who had entered the country had come to stay. So had Theravada Buddhism, which reached Rakhine by way of Sri Lanka, South India and South Myanmar.

Over the centuries, the physiognomy of the Rakhinese people also changed. The racial mixture of Indo-Europeans with the only recently-arrived Central Asians became predominantly Mongoloid, an ethnic mixture that still characterizes today's Rakhine people. The five centuries that followed the arrival of the Tibeto-Burmans in Rakhine were an age of darkness when the region became a powerless tributary of Bagan and Innwa (Ava). It was only after the country turned again towards the West during the 15th century that a cultural renaissance began, inspiring the heyday of Rakhine's medieval history.

*Islamic influences.* By the 13th century, Islam had conquered the hearts and the souls of the people who lived between Africa's Atlantic seaboard and Bengal, and disseminated the most powerful set of values of the age. Not unexpectedly, the Buddhist kingdom of Rakhine drew its new life through the aid and assistance of the Islamic ruler of Gaur. This Bengali sovereign reinstated King Narameikhla to his rightful throne in the year 1430. Since that time, all the kings of Rakhine have carried an Islamic title in addition to their Buddhist designation.

*Living on the river.*

Twenty-four years earlier, Narameikhla had been ousted by the Innwa Dynasty and he had spent the intervening years at the Gaur court learning revolutionary ideas in the fields of mathematics and natural sciences which, together with a monotheistic belief, had fostered the success of Islam. Asia's feudal caste-oriented societies could offer no lasting resistance to these ideas, and were unable to halt the eastward surge of this formidable alliance of faith and knowledge. Rakhine was to profit from it all. Unlike the Myanmar kingdom, it welcomed the new perspectives.

From the Portuguese, who appeared in the coastal waters during the 16th century, the inhabitants of Rakhine acquired the art of seafaring. Within a very short time, the whole coast from Chittagong to Bago (Pegu) was under their control. They traded with the Lusitanians, the Danish and the Dutch, and until the year 1666 they

83

bravely withstood the mighty Mogul Empire from which they had snatched the southern part of Bengal. It was a time of magic and miracles, of splendor and grandeur. But this was only one side of the story. The seafaring Rakhine people, together with the Portuguese half-castes who had settled south of Chittagong, were also known as *Maghs*. These seafarers and half-castes were a race of pirates and slave traders who terrorized the peaceful population of the Ganga Delta region.

It was during this time that the sad story of Shah Shuja came to its tragic climax at Mrauk-U Rakhine's splendid capital. Shuja was the rightful heir to the Mogul throne but he was cheated and defeated by his vicious brother Aurangzeb. Sanda-thu-dhamma, the King of Rakhine, granted him asylum; this benevolent gesture, however, was only meant to deceive Shuja. In fact, Sanda-thu-dhamma was after Shuja's beautiful daughter and the immeasurable treasures he carried with him. When Shuja, in whose eyes the Rakhine king was only a Magh warlord, refused to give his daughter in marriage, he and his retinue were cold-bloodedly slaughtered. Shuja's daughters of course ended up in Sanda-thu-dhamma's harem, but when the latter found he was unable to break their Mogul pride he had the girls executed within a year.

*The power of magic.* Brahman astrologers and runic scientists protected Rakhine throughout these centuries of power with the medieval magical art of *yadaya*. Its purpose was to put the hidden powers of the micro- and macrocosm at the disposal of the court. This was accomplished with incantations and bells, which – ringing at astronomically predetermined times and places – drove frightened enemies from the country, made kings invincible, and protected the land from natural disasters. The chronicles tell of many such incidents. Buddhist cosmology, medieval Islamic sciences and ancient Brahman rituals gave 17th-century Rakhine its unique character. The mood of the time and the exotic setting of the place were unprecedented in human history. Friar Manrique tells the story of King Thiri-thu-dhamma's elixir of immortality that a Muslim doctor brewed for the superstitious monarch. According to Manrique, the doctor used the essence of the hearts of 2,000 white doves, 4,000 white cows and 6,000 humans. It seems not to have worked. Thiri-thu-dhamma, entangled in palace intrigues, was poisoned by an elixir even stronger.

If we imagine Rakhine today as it was then, we should not allow today's values to blur the image. Rakhine was enjoying an intriguing and fascinating era and its magic-ridden peculiarities arose from the clash and cross-fertilization of opposing cultures. Indeed, the magic of *yadaya* was so powerful that it was only by adapting incantations and magic ritual to their own purposes that the Myanmars put an end to Rakhine's invulnerability in 1784. They achieved this by dismantling the sacred Maha Muni and carrying it over the Rakhine Yoma to Amarapura where it was to work the same portentous magic for the kings of Myanmar. After that, Rakhine's history as an independent kingdom came to an end.

A Westerner might think that this belief in magic must have vanished with the approach of modern times. Not so in Myanmar. Only a few decades ago, in the 1930s, a peasant rebellion against the British was brewing on the other side of the Rakhine Yoma. Its leader, Saya San, also called Thupannaka Galon Raja, was crowned by the rebels in a traditional ceremony as the new king of Burma. The British knew nothing about it until they found themselves facing an unusual armed uprising. Saya San's troops prepared for battle in the traditional Myanmar way. Maurice Collis, then an official in British-Burma, describes what happened.

*One day, Shwe Yon addressed the rebel forces from a dais whereon was a heap of swords, a pile of amulets and beside him a gong. He said: 'I now give you amulets*

*Durian vendors.*

*which will render you sword- and gun-proof. In the case of this gong, it has magic power. Wish for what you want and sound this gong. When you meet government troops, sound it and they will be stupefied. Sound it and their arms will flow away like the water of a river; sound it, advance and cut them down.'* Advance they did, fearlessly confronting British machine-gun positions with home-made swords and muskets. The outcome was a predictable massacre.

*Superstition.* In Sandoway, a Rakhine coastal city called *Dvaravati* in ancient times, there are three pagodas, the Andaw, the Nandaw and the Sandaw. All of them enshrine relics of Buddha's former incarnations, and they stand at an angle to each other forming a perfect magico-astrological diagram.

People living within this diagram's perimeter are convinced they live on sacred soil and thus feel protected from the evil that abounds in the world. If you ask them, they also believe in what is written in one of the *Jatakas*, that *Dvaravati* can rise up and hover above the ground when attacked by an enemy. Though we might smile when we hear such a story, the truth is that for most of the inhabitants who have ever lived here, this has not been proven wrong. Their belief in it has made their lives comfortable and free of doubts. Surely, our situation, based on our own "religion" of science, is not much different. Sometime in the future, someone might sit and smile when he learns of the righteousness with which we defended the empirical views of our time. Rakhine, with its superstitious past and present, can still teach us.

*On the way to fetch water.*

*Modern times.* In 1824, when the British annexed Rakhine during the First Anglo-Burmese War, Rakhine's doors were again flung wide open towards India, as they had been over 1,000 years earlier. During the subsequent colonial period, landless Muslim immigrants from Bengal came and settled freely in the country. Many of them stayed after Myanmar's independence, transforming the ethnic and political landscape of the province. There is still some enmity between the Myanmars and the predominantly Mongolian inhabitants of Rakhine, though ultimately they speak a similar language, profess the same religion, and live identical lives. The real antagonism in today's Rakhine exists between the many pure-blooded Bengalis, the Rohingyas, who constitute the bulk of the Muslim citizenry, and the Tibeto-Burman Buddhist majority.

The Rakhines cherish their ancestral relationship with the inhabitants of the Ayeyarwady valley. They see themselves as Myanmars, as members of a Southeast Asian nation that borders on South Asia. As secluded as Rakhine is today, connected to the outside world only via Yangon, it looks east again.

85

**B**efore the fog fades, the undulating countryside
of Rakhine reveals its fairy-tale features.

Indra, the Vedic god, has gone through many
metamorphoses. In Buddhist India he became Sakka,
in Myanmar he is Thagyamin, the king of the *nats*.

91

**H**igh-wheeled ox carts trail dust and mud behind them as they ramble around the villages.

**R**akhinese islanders are a race of expert sailors.

**A** multitude of creeks, rivers and canals
act as Rakhine's main transport arteries.

97

The *nat* that lives in this Launggyet tree
will never have to move as long as the inhabitants
of the area continue to bow to him in reverence.

99

**S**imple gadgets enhance the beauty of the people.

*An early poster of a " giraffe woman.*"

*A Shan poet.*

*Working in the field after the rain.*

*Playing the Myanmar harp.*

**B**irth after birth, over and again,
With dirt and besmirching,
Oppression and evil,
Fading and withering,
Longing and craving,
Panting and gasping,
Sobbing and weeping,
Toil and weariness,
All pervading round and round
Like a spinning wheel.

*Samsara, Ko-gan Pyo*

**E**very year, during the Myanmar month of *Thadingyut* (September/October), the Southern Shan State hosts a unique championship. Participants are young men from the 200 villages fringing Lake Inle, Myanmar's most picturesque body of fresh water. These Intha tribesmen compete in the famous "leg-rowing" regatta where their eel-like boats must be propelled by the power of their leg muscles only.

The Inthas are a tribe of 70,000 who originally lived in the Dawei (Tavoy) region of Tanintharyi (Tenasserim). Their own tradition tells that they began migrating to this lake district as early as the 14th century. Most probably they only completed their resettlement at Inle during the 18th century when their homeland was ravaged by the continuous wars between the Siamese and the Myanmars.

The Inthas' story is a picture-book example of human adaptability, of man's ability to survive in the face of seemingly insurmountable odds, and this theme is as topical today in the mountains of Myanmar as it was a thousand years ago. The Inthas' success story is one of a very few. When they left their Daweian homeland as a small tribe and resettled in this far-off mountain region, they had to acquire a totally new set of cultural survival techniques.

*Floating gardens.* The men became fishermen whose unparalleled way of rowing their boats and unique conical fish traps are to be found nowhere else in the world. Their wives' floating gardens are equally unique. Since the land fronting the lake belonged to the Shans – the original inhabitants of this area – when the Inthas

*A Shan princess with her servants.*

arrived, they had to settle literally on the surface of the lake. There they constructed their own gardens on the water. They matted dried reeds, covered them with muck scooped from the lake bottom, and anchored these 6x330-foot (2x100-meter) floating gardens with bamboo poles in the shallow lake around their stilt houses. Today, the Inthas are Myanmar's foremost vegetable growers and flower gardeners. Their technique has its equivalent only in the Mexican highlands where a similar way of floating gardening was independently developed by the Aztecs. The Inthas' prosperity is in stark contrast to the conditions under which most other small hill-tribes live. Myanmar's ethnic composition, as in all of Southeast Asia, displays evidence of the universal human struggle for better land and better living conditions that every generation tries to produce for its offspring.

*Markets and festivals.* For visitors to Myanmar, the city of Taunggyi offers the best chance to see some of its numerous tribes. A shifting market comes to the city every fifth day. On this day, the town beneath the "big mountain", from where it gets its name, offers a rare spectacle of psychedelic-colored dresses and costumes. Tribal folk from the remotest mountain hamlets come here to trade and shop, to see and be seen. As these isolated villages have been cut off from the rest of the world for decades, you will find inquisitive women and children gazing longingly at goods and trinkets from the world beyond their valley. Since the opening of the road from Thailand to Kengtung, Western influence has infiltrated the remote hilltribes.

There is another remarkable market at Ywama on Lake Inle, around 17 miles (27 km) by road and 1,800 feet (550 meters) downhill from Taunggyi. The peculiarity of the market stems from the fact that it takes place on the lake; buyers and shoppers move around in small boats, doing their deals across the boards of their rocking crafts. This market has the special flavor that Bangkok's floating market had more than 30 years ago.

*Kayin girls in their national dress.*

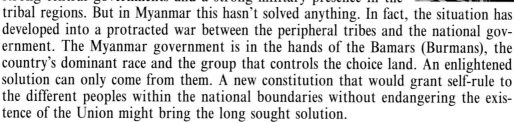

*An ancient conflict.* Migrations, tribal conflicts, regional upheavals and civil wars were always part of daily life between the Himalayas and the South China Sea. Today, we must add the environmental catastrophe that results from over-population and the consequent depletion of the forests and the topsoil. To date, the only solution offered for such conflicts has been the creation of strong central governments and a strong military presence in the tribal regions. But in Myanmar this hasn't solved anything. In fact, the situation has developed into a protracted war between the peripheral tribes and the national government. The Myanmar government is in the hands of the Bamars (Burmans), the country's dominant race and the group that controls the choice land. An enlightened solution can only come from them. A new constitution that would grant self-rule to the different peoples within the national boundaries without endangering the existence of the Union might bring the long sought solution.

*Sharing the land.* The geographical distribution of Myanmar's tribes is a schoolbook example of the natural law by which the best land goes to the strongest people. The irrigated plain of Central Myanmar and the Ayeyarwady River valley are inhabited by the Bamars. They share the coastal area and the prime rice-growing region of the Ayeyarwady Delta with the lowland Karen. After the Second World War, this land was all but confiscated by the *Chettyars*, a caste of South Indian money-lenders who understood nothing about growing rice but knew perfectly well how capitalism works. The Bamars reacted with a *coup d'etat* which drove the Indians out of Myanmar and resulted in a redistribution of land to the dominant groups. However, continuous pressure is still exerted today by the people who remained in the hills. They too know the value of land "where a mere tickling of the ground answers with a golden harvest," as George Scott once commented.

A migratory trend towards the more fertile lower elevation is still taking place: for example, a group of Karen has settled in the Delta region that was only opened to cultivation during the British period. But most of the non-Tibeto-Burman speaking peoples are still entrenched in the hills.

*The Shans.* Numbering about 3.2 million, the Shans constitute the second largest ethnic group in Myanmar. The Bamars know what that means. After the fall of Bagan, the Shans – whose name in Chinese means "mountain people" – descended from the hills and tried to evict the Bamars from their new-found homeland. The struggle went on for centuries, and even though the Shans had the upper hand in the beginning, the Bamars finally succeeded in repossessing the fertile fields of Central Myanmar. One subdivision of the Shans had more luck: they moved down the Menam valley on the other side of the mountains separating Myanmar and Thailand. There they settled amidst the Mon-Khmer speaking inhabitants of the region and founded the Siamese nation that we now know as Thailand.

In Myanmar, the Shans had to settle on the undulating eastern plateau and along the river valleys that cut through the mountains. Until a few decades ago they were split into 34 feudal principalities, each one headed by a hereditary prince – a so-called *sawbwa* – who ruled in a medieval fashion. Like the Bamars, the Shans are Buddhists but, being located away from the centers of learning in Myanmar, their leaning towards animism is much stronger than in the lowlands.

*Animistic tribes.* As they are closer to the powers of nature, the tribes in the hills share their lives with the animistic spirits that abound in the air, the water and the soil. They feel their presence in everything that is startling or extraordinary, everything that is beyond simple explanation.

103

The rituals that they have developed to appease the spirits, though outwardly showing Buddhist colors, can easily be traced to their Shamanist forefathers. Their view on procreation illustrates this queer mixture of Buddhist rationalism with ancient animism:

> *Pregnancy cannot be caused by mere men;*
> *The child is his when at the time of intercourse*
> *Three causes combine,*
> *And the three causes are:*
> *The proper season of the woman,*
> *Copulation with a man,*
> *The release of a fate by the death of some animated being...*
> *The fate may be released from any being in the animal kingdom,*
> *A human being for example.*
> *In its fast orbit around the earth it searches for a new home*
> *Where a woman in season is combining with a man,*
> *This is where the fate is fated to come to rest.*

Whatever an animist is about to do that is of importance – building a house, plowing or sowing a field, starting a journey or marrying off his children – he will

invariably start with a propitiation of the relevant *nats*. These *nats* are not the national *nats*, neither are they the inhabitants of heavenly abodes, nor funny gnomes; these animistic *nats* can be quite vicious and they do whatever they want. Only by offering them food or other useful things can one propitiate them. Nothing could be more opposed to the essence of Theravada Buddhism as this belief in *nat*, but in the Myanmar backwoods, as elsewhere, religion is a peculiar mixture of ritual and doctrine. This is why *pongyis* take part in these superstitious rites; some of them are also expert astrologers, tattooers and fortune-tellers.

*Padaung women, known as the "giraffe women", at the turn of the century.*

*The village nat.* All communities have their particular village *nat* who lives somewhere in a quiet grove or mighty tree near the hamlet. Normally he is left in peace and people carefully walk around his habitat so as not to disturb him or give him reason to become enraged. Sometimes, however, when deficient rainfall, a delay in the monsoon rains or other common natural afflictions befall the village, the whole population moves out to the hallowed spot where the *nat* lives and conduct a formal service.

This service is performed by one of the revered village elders who offers rice, fowl, eggs, rice spirit and pickled tea to the *nat*, followed by a libation of water, whereupon the elder will pray to the *nat* to grant the village relief from its ills. The villagers all contribute to these offerings, then genuflect as they do at a pagoda. But since these *nats* are not compassionate in any sense, they have to also propitiate all the other *nats* in the vicinity with similar offerings so they will not become jealous and counteract the village's own *nat*.

*The truth lies in the intestines.* In spite of the Buddhist precept that "thou shalt not kill," a chicken is sacrificed and the entrails are examined. The bigger the intestines and the stomach, the more likely it is that the villagers' request will be answered. Though this seems irrational and superstitious behavior, if you look at it from an anthropologist's point of view, you can see it has sensible origins. When all these tribes were moving south, they came across unknown seeds and berries, roots and leaves, not knowing if they were poisonous or healthy. So they fed their livestock

with whatever food was unfamiliar to them. By checking the size and color of the heart, the liver, the stomach and the intestines, these forefathers of today's hill-tribes were able to determine the quality of the foodstuffs they found. At that time, a chicken's death really helped to find an answer to an unfamiliar phenomenon of nature, but today it has degenerated into a pure ritual. Most contemporary and seemingly incomprehensible rites were often once carried out for practical reasons.

Some of today's tribes are still steadfast animists who do not even pretend to be Buddhists. They have had little contact with the outside world and live on the remotest slopes and ridges in the Shan and Kachin hills bordering Laos and China. They make up the third and least developed collection of Myanmar's manifold races. Some 126 ethnically or culturally distinct groups have been identified in Myanmar, speaking 242 separate languages and dialects. The most numerous of them – the Shans, Karens, Mon, Kachins, Chins and Rakhinese – all have their own state and, according to the now defunct 1974 constitution, a certain autonomy. Some of them maintain clandestine armies that are trying to break away from the Union and from Bamar overlordship.

*Cycles of destruction.* Most small tribes cannot tell a success story similar to that of the Inthas. Theirs is a hard and burdensome life. Their crops don't just grow by *"tickling the earth"*; in the hills, rice, maize, millet, buckwheat, beans, sesame and cotton must be grown by slash-and burn agriculture, one of the most work-intensive methods of planting cereals and vegetables.

Once a piece of virgin forest has been chosen as future cropland, the trees are felled and burned. The ground is then plowed, harrowed and sown, with ashes fertilizing the ground shortly before the monsoonal rains break. Even with scientific crop rotation, these fields are depleted after three or four years, so a new piece of land must be cleared since the now-exhausted soil needs at least 10 to 12 years to recuperate. Fields therefore must be moved further and further away from the dwellings, until finally the village itself has to move to a more central location.

*Where tears are growing.* It is no wonder the tribes search for new ways to feed their growing population. They have profited most from the planting of a cash crop that is in such great demand that it earns enough money for the tribesmen to buy food from the market; this cash crop is the poppy, or more specifically the tears of the poppy, also called *papaver somniferum* or opium.

By observing the hill country of eastern and northern Myanmar, you can see why some tribes developed into strong nations while others remained stagnant for centuries without the prospect of becoming independent nations. The forces of history are the same today in northeast Myanmar as they were during the Neolithic Age. In those days, however, there were only few people and a seemingly limitless and wide world. Today, there is little arable land available, and the population continues to grow every day. The Bamars and the Shans were the last of the tribes to find their "promised land" some 800 to 1,000 years ago. Their growth from small tribes to large nations is beyond the scope of the inhabitants of the remote mountains.

**105**

*A Shan in his traditional outfit.*

**A** fishing fleet, suspended on its own reflection.

**T**he depth of Lake Inle does not exceed 10 feet
(three meters). Inthas employ special techniques in
fishing there.

111

**T**he Inthas of Lake Inle migrated from the Tanintharyi region into the hills to start a tranquil and prosperous new life.

113

**T**he shifting market that comes every fifth day to Taunggyi is a feast of food and fun. Members of most of the hill tribes are found in attendance.

**C**urry and chilies are condiments
for the peasant's palate.

The towel is the Shan's headdress.

*C*heroots are still made by hand...

117

... and then bundled for the market.

**T**he *cheroot* is as typical of the true Myanmar
as the cup of tea is of an Englishman.

**T**he Shans are the majority race in the hills and are
closely related to the Thais on the other side of the border.

123

An Intha poles a newly acquired garden across the lake.

A floating garden and an Intha leg-rower exemplify the ingenious adaptability hill tribes have developed during their centuries of migration.

*On the terrace of the Shwedagon 170 years ago.*

*The Maha Gandhara bell.*

To give to monks a dwelling place,
Wherein in safety and at ease
To think and insight gain
The Buddha praises most of all.
Let therefore a wise man,
Regarding his own weal,
Have pleasant monasteries built,
And lodge there learned men.
Give food to them and drink,
And clothes and dwelling places
To the upright in mind.
Then they shall preach to him the Norm
– The Norm dispelling every grief –
Which Norm, when here he learns,
He sins no more,
Reaching the perfect well.

*Vinaya, Chullavagga VI, 1*

*View of Yangon in 1825.*

*A park in Yangon at the end of the 19th century.*

**A**t a time when the ancestors of the Bamars had barely left their Gansu homeland, the Mon – another tribe from the windswept plains of Central Asia – had already reached the alluvial plain along the gulfs of Siam and Martaban; though they too were not the first ones to settle there. Fifteen thousand years earlier, a long-forgotten race had domesticated the wild growing rice paddies and established humanity's first agricultural civilization in this region.

When the "Ramans," as the Mon called themselves, arrived in their land of destiny, they founded a kingdom they proudly called the "Land of Gold." It is not difficult to see where this name originated. You only have to see the paddies at harvest time, when the coastal plain beneath the mountains is submerged in a sea of gold, to find the answer. This also answers the question of why this fertile stretch of land has had a magnetic attraction for so many races.

*A romanticized landscape as seen in an age before photography.*

This kingdom was a loose federation of three states on either side of the Tanintharyi (Tenasserim) Range. In the east was *Haripunjaya* in what is now northern Thailand and the legendary kingdom of *Dvaravati*, located near modern Lopburi. West of the watershed lay *Thaton*, the ancient capital of the Myanmar Mon-land.

For 1,000 years, the Mon were the unchallenged rulers of that land. They became Southeast Asia's most cultured people. The surviving art and architecture speak of an era of peace, prosperity and deep religious feelings. While other tribes that live today in Myanmar were still bogged down in a Neolithic culture, *Suvannabhumi*, the ancient "Golden Land," was already a part of Greater India. It shared the wisdom and social development of the Mauryan and Kushan Empires on the subcontinent. All of Southeast Asia could have become the domain of the Mon, who had the knowledge and the opportunity open to those who arrive first. But they were not a warrior race: they were a race of poets. Similar to the deep religiosity that is inherent in Romanesque artifacts of medieval Europe, the art of the Mon exudes compassion and a heartwarming simplicity, as is demonstrated by what still remains of their culture today.

*Nursing the Buddha.* We know from many sources that Suvannabhumi was a Buddhist kingdom. The oldest written records speak of two merchant brothers from Okkala who offered Gautama Buddha his first meal after the seven-week-long meditation that followed his Enlightenment. In exchange for this kindness they received eight hairs of the Exalted One. They carried them to their ruler King Okkalapa, who had a stupa built on Singuttara Hill, just above what is today's Yangon. In the *Thamaing Athit*, the chronicle of the Shwedagon, the founding ceremony of this stupa is described in a traditional poetic way:

> *When Sakka opened the ruby casket*
> *To take out the hairs to be washed,*
> *The hairs flew up to a height of seven palm trees,*
> *And rays of many colors emanated from them.*
> *The Petas could see the men,*
> *And the men could see the ghosts.*
> *The blind recovered their sight.*
> *The dumb could speak.*
> *The crippled regained their strength.*
> *The earth and the water shook.*

128

*The Meru bent its head.*
*The seven ranges shook together.*
*Sheet lightning and forked lightning played in the sky.*
*A rain of jewels fell.*
*Trees bore fruit and flowers bore blossoms out of season.*

Over the centuries, Shwedagon became Buddhism's most venerated shrine, a gold-covered wonder of architecture, an edifice that incorporates everything that is genuine in Myanmar, a place of exaltation and awe, a gilded spot in the landscape that can be seen with the naked eye from a plane 39,000 feet (12,000 meters) up in the air. The Shwedagon alone is reason enough to visit Myanmar. A description of its exterior, however, will unavoidably give the impression of a somewhat gaudy Buddhist Disneyland, but this is only the outward appearance of something that is much more profound.

*The Golden Glory.* Apart from all the gold and glitter, the exotic architecture of the *tazaungs* and *chedis*, the images, paintings and mythological beings that surround you on the Shwedagon's stairways and platform, there is such a pious air about the place, such beauty in the movements of the people who come to pray that the atmosphere is almost that of a high-columned Gothic cathedral. Here, however, the ceiling of this religious edifice is the sky, or in this context, the heavens. If you identify the seemingly endless wealth of astrological symbols, mythological beings and Buddhist stories on the platform, you will realize that this is a display of all of humanity's fears and longings, transformed into wood, plaster and stone.

Moving up one level above the main platform brings you above the sphere of *Kama Loka*; here you leave the "Pagoda Buddhism" of the lay people behind you. In the tranquillity that encompasses the stupa's upper base you'll find the future "stream enterers," dwarfed and engulfed by the gold leaf covering of the huge *chedi*, in deep *jhanic* meditation; these are men whose aspirations are no longer of this world. Fortunately, not everyone is permitted to go up, though it is here that Myanmar's timeless strengths can best be felt. The seclusion of this place, just one layer above the free-flowing mass of people on the main platform, is something intensely symbolic. If the Shwedagon is intended to be a symbol of the Buddhist cosmos, then this upper layer also exemplifies the contrast between *Kama Loka* and *Arupa Loka* and shows how deeply these people believe in the existence of the Buddhist universe. Once on the Shwedagon, you should not forget that this ground has been sacred for more than 2,500 years, that generation after generation has come up here to reinforce its belief, and that today it thrives with the same intensity it has had from time immemorial.

**129**

*The Mon under pressure.* It was back in the 3rd century BC that the Mauryan king Ashoka sent two elders, Sona and Uttara, to *Suvannabhumi* to propagate the Buddhist gospel. Outside *Thaton* they built the Kelasa Monastery from which the eternal truth of the *dhamma* spread throughout mainland Southeast Asia. Great changes came after the middle of the first millennium AD when Hinduism regained dominance in India, and when Brahmans and traders, the true conveyers of Indian culture, brought Hindu and Mahayana ideas to foreign shores. Soon after, the T'ang dynasty fell in China and a variety of tribes moved towards the south and began applying intensive pressure on the Mons along the golden coast. Within a few centuries, *Thaton* had fallen to the Bamars, *Dvaravati* to the Khmers, and

*A view of Yangon towards the southeast after the First Anglo-Burmese War.*

*British soldiers marching on the road to the Shwedagon in 1825.*

*Haripunjaya* to the Tai-Shans. The Mon became sandwiched in their own homeland between the immigrants from the west and the invaders from the north. East of the Tanintharyi mountain range, the Mon vanished as a political entity, absorbed into the Siamese and Khmer kingdoms. But this was not so on the Myanmar side, for very soon after Anawrahta's conquest of *Thaton*, the conquerors were sitting at the feet of the vanquished.

Among the pupils of the Mon was King Kyanzittha, the very monarch who had subjugated them and established a Myanmar supremacy that was to last as long as the Bagan kingdom flourished. Kyanzittha favored Mon architecture; his inscriptions were in the Mon language; and his romantic love affair with the daughter of the king of Bago (Pegu) is a popular theme on Myanmar's stages today. The Mon taught the Bamars what they themselves had learned from the Indians, and in return the pious strength of the Bagan kingdom preserved the orthodoxy of their Theravada Buddhism.

*The heyday of the Mon.* From 1287 to 1539, during a two and a half century period, as long as the life-span of the Bagan empire, *Ramanadesa* represented Myanmar to the outside world. This kingdom had its ups and downs, but Bago's most glorious period was not a time of expansion and wars. Neither was it a time of dominance over other people. Instead, Bago is remembered for a century-long era of peace and prosperity based, not on the spoils of war and slave trade, but on the industriousness and labor of its own people. Shinsawbu, the beloved queen of this era, gave the Shwedagon its present form; she died with her eyes fixed on the glorious golden structure. To her it symbolized the existence of the three worlds of man, *devas* and *brahmas*. As a devout Buddhist queen she was sure to be reborn in one of the higher celestial abodes. (After the British conquest of Lower Myanmar, the Mon spread the word that Queen Victoria was a new incarnation of Shinsawbu.)

**130**

*The zawgyi king.* Queen Shinsawbu installed as her successor Dhammazedi, a learned monk who was also a *zawgyi* – an alchemist and master of runes. He had the universal knowledge of his time. According to traditional folklore, Dhammazedi and his companion, Dhammapala, were two monks who taught Shinsawbu when she was still a Mon princess married to the king of Innwa (Ava). But she was unhappy and fled with her two tutors back to Bago. Many years later, when her life was nearing its end, the queen was in a dilemma over which of her two loyal instructors should marry her daughter and become successor to the throne.

*The war of the runes.* Dhammazedi was finally chosen, but Dhammapala, also a master of the runes, was envious, and secretly plotted against the new king. He studied the runes long and hard, and finally found what he was searching for. If he could stay buried under the earth unmolested for seven days, all the hidden powers of the universe would be at his disposal. But Dhammazedi, who knew that his former companion was on the verge of success, had Dhammapala's apprentice tortured until his master's burial-place was revealed and virtually at the last minute before the

*A rice barge on the Yangon River.*

appointed time had been completed, Dhammapala was dug up. Dhammazedi was thus able to deny him his life and his supreme knowledge. Had the victorious magician eaten a piece of his rival's corpse, he would have gained the ultimate truth himself, but Dhammazedi abstained. It is said that later he rediscovered the ultimate runes himself, but he used their power only to be a righteous king. While the story is folklore, it is a historical fact that Dhammazedi had the plotting Dhammapala executed.

The court, however, was not satisfied with the new king, since Dhammazedi was not of royal blood and thus not eligible for the throne. So Shinsawbu had an image of Buddha cut out of the beam of a bridge and she said:

*"Ye say he is of common blood, he cannot be your king. See here this common wood, yesterday it was trodden in the dust of your feet, but today, is it not the Lord and do you not bow before it?"*

Chronicles also reveal that Dhammazedi was the king who sent monks to Sri Lanka for valid ordination. It is only through this ordination – still the backbone of today's *sangha* – that every young monk learns the names of his teachers' teachers, all the way back to Gautama himself. After Dhammazedi, the decline of *Ramanadesa* set in. In 1539, the kingdom was incorporated into the Second Myanmar Empire; the Mon of today still look back with sadness at its passing. The Mon did make one more attempt in the 18th century to reclaim power, but Alaungpaya, the charismatic Bamar leader from Shwebo, conclusively ended the dream of an independent *Ramanadesa*. Those Mon who did not flee after the fall of Bago were assimilated by the Bamars. It was Alaungpaya who then renamed Dagon, calling it Yangon, "End of Strife," to commemorate the final decline of Mon power.

*The Golden Rock.* To travel in the Karen-dominated region of South Myanmar along the Thai border is rather difficult nowadays, since the Karen are fighting a protracted war with the Bamars. They have their own government institutions in the jungle along the border, their own army, schools, hospitals and border posts. Their weapons are financed with the tax they exact on smuggled goods that have to be carried across their territory to reach the markets in Myanmar proper. Though the famous Golden Rock, deep in the mountains of Tanintharyi to the east of the small town of Kyaikto, lies in the heart of the Karen territory, this area is designated as "brown," meaning there is no imminent danger of fighting between government and rebel troops. Visits, therefore, are sometimes possible. The Kyaik-tyio Pagoda, as the natives call it, is peculiar in that in spite of its size and weight (18 feet/5.5 meters in diameter) you can rock it with your bare hands. It seems that it will at any minute tumble down the steep precipice atop which it is located, though locals will tell you that this is impossible. Like the Shwedagon, this rock contains a hair of the Buddha, and this hair supposedly keeps it balanced.

If you stay overnight in one of the nearby rest houses, you will have the opportunity to see the rock in the early morning when it appears and disappears between the fast moving clouds sweeping in from the coast. This almost mystical scene brings to mind Myanmar Buddhist paintings and drawings that depict the slopes of Mount Meru, the heavenly abode of spirits and gods.

The Golden Rock would be a tourist attraction of the first order were it not located so deep in the jungle of Tanintharyi. Like so many other places in Myanmar, it belongs to a mystical landscape that resembles the visions the mind produces when contemplating ancient Buddhist fables and legends. Its seclusion has saved it from becoming a commodity of the tourist industry, and there is a faint chance that coming generations might still get a glimpse of the meaning that lies behind its unique beauty.

*On the terrace of the Shwedagon at the turn of the century.*

133

**T**he Golden Pagoda, Yangon's Shwedagon,
looks back on a 2,500-year-history.

**S**ixty-four shrines with golden finials
encircle the octagonal base of the stupa.

**S**tupas, *tazaungs*, *pyathats* and *Tagundaings*,
all assist in lifting the soul of the pious toward the
infinite, the universal *dhamma*.

**A** modern Myanmar girl who is unwilling
to concede that "religion is the opium of the people".

139

**"I** take refuge in the Buddha,
I take refuge in the Dhamma,
I take refuge in the Sangha.**"**
*The Three Jewels, the Buddhist's prayer*

**F**lowers and faith go hand in hand.

143

**P**agoda spires sometimes look like radio antennae
set up to receive messages from another world.

The Ayeyarwady steamers, though battered and aged, remain a mainstay of transport.

147

They are an ever-smiling race,
even though they often carry a heavy load.

**M**odern utensils are like modern ideas,
streamlined and shiny for a faster turnover.

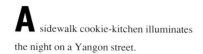

**A** sidewalk cookie-kitchen illuminates the night on a Yangon street.

**S**elling after-dinner treats al fresco: a *cheroot* and betel-nut stand.

**T**he traditional Myanmar dress
blends new and old with a certain charm.

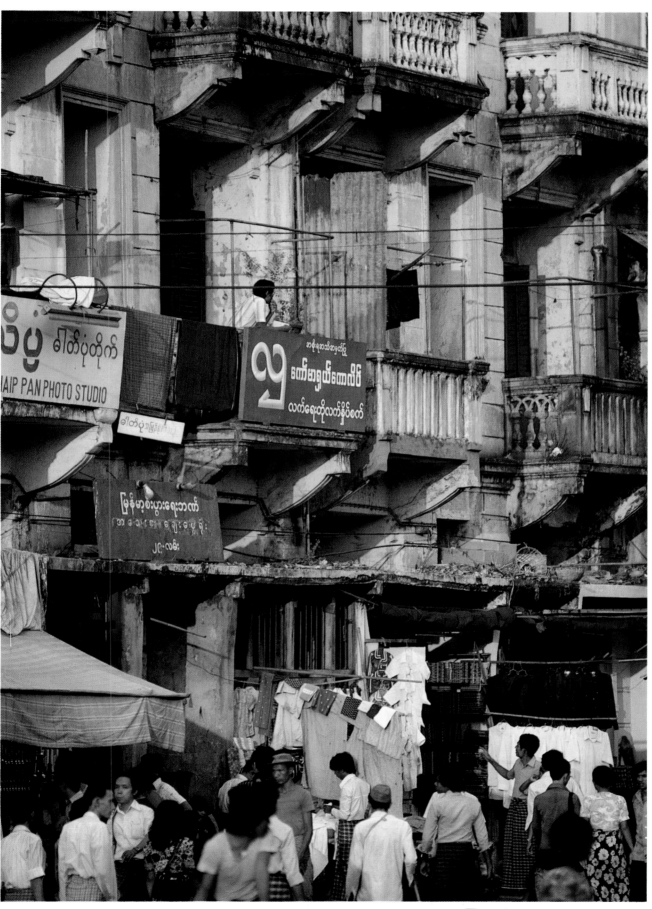

**D**owntown Yangon has changed only
marginally since the 1930s.

153

**M**any of the delta rice mills
are run and owned by Chinese families.

**C**onstant exposure to the elements has left its mark
on the faces of the people working the paddy fields.

157

The old and the new, the eternal and the disposable, are seen in the face of contemporary Myanmar, symbolized by this Sule Pagoda Buddha.

**T**he balance of the Golden Rock – and that
of the country as a whole – is maintained
by the strong belief in Buddhism.

How transient are all component things!
Their nature's to be born and die;
Coming they go; and then is best,
When each has ceased, and all is rest!

As rivers when they fill must flow,
And reach and fill the distant main;
So surely what is given here
Will reach and bless the spirits there!
If you on earth will gladly give
Departed ghosts will gladly live!

As water poured on mountain tops
Must soon descend and reach the plain;
So surely what is given here
Will reach and bless the spirits there!

*Maha-Parinibbana Sutta.*

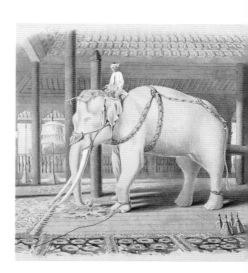

Back at the beginning of the 1980s, **Pfannmüller** and **Klein,** the creators of this book, were moving in and out of Myanmar (then Burma) to collect additional text and pictures for the *Insight Guide Burma.* It was then that **Hans Höfer,** the publisher of Apa Publications' Insight Guides, realized that these authors had collected material that demanded an alternative approach. He asked both of them to continue compilation, working towards a book that would reveal what a practical guide-book could not: that which is invisible to the bare eyes; the beauty that comes only through an intimate knowledge of its sources and its roots; the atmosphere that generates a smile.

The photographer Pfannmüller and the writer Klein already made an ideal team. They knew each other well from many trips all over Asia. Both of them were spellbound by the country, and they soon realized that they understood what they saw not only through their senses but also with their hearts. The book became a labor of love and they took their time to complete it to their own satisfaction. In 1993/94 they went to Myanmar for six weeks. Due to the peace accord with the Kachins they were permitted to visit the confluence of Meikha and Malikha, the origin of the Ayeyarwady and go by boat along the entire river.

Both Pfannmüller and Klein were fortunate in the assistance of *Myanmar Travels & Tours.* Especially valuable was the assistance of **U Thaw Dar Sein, U Myo Lwin** and **U Khin Kyaw.** Special thanks must go to **U Win Aung** who, despite difficult times, understood Pfannmüller and Klein's vision of the book and helped in its realization. They did their best to arrange trips to areas that are beyond the normal tourist's itinerary. It is due to their dedication that tourism to Myanmar is again picking up during trying times. However, for them, as for the authors of this book, the question of whether tourism can help to improve the life of the people of Myanmar remains unanswered. Perhaps this book will promote an understanding of the situation by making some of the invisible traits discernible to the uninitiated.

*Burma the Golden* went to print thanks to the additional interest of a German and an English publishing house that wanted a book which acquaints westerners with the enduring face of Myanmar. Both Pfannmüller and Klein sat down to finalize the book, adding new material and supplementing it with some 50 historical slides from Klein's substantial photo archive of ancient Myanmar views.

In 1993 they were joined by **V. Barl,** Apa Publications' art director. Barl, a native of Slovenia who teaches at the Krefeld Academy of Design, created the layout of the book so that Pfannmüller's photos could present their message in an unobstructed way. The Apa production crew, with **Andrew Eames** in London and **Dieter Vogel** in Munich, gave the book its final touches.

**161**

# A

*Alaungpaya–* the founder of the Third Myanmar Empire (1752-1760).

*Alaungsithu–* the fourth king of the Bagan Dynasty (1112-1167). One of Bagan's most pious kings, at the age of 81 he was smothered by his son Narathu.

*Amarapura–* was founded in 1781 as the capital of Myanmar, then in 1823 the capital moved to Innwa. However, it became Myanmar's capital once more between 1837 and 1860.

*Ananda Temple–* built by Kyanzittha in imitation of the cave temple of Ananta in the Udayagiri hills of India.

*anatta–* "non-self" or non-personality, one of the three traits of existence.

*Anawrahta–* (1044-1077) also called Aniruddha, founder of the First Myanmar Empire. He was gored by a wild buffalo in 1077 when returning from one of his conquests.

*anicca–* impermanence in Pali.

*Aparagoyana–* the westernmost island of the Buddhist cosmos.

*Arimaddana–* the "City of the Enemy Crusher," Bagan's classical name.

*Ari-monks–* pre-Bagan Brahman teachers who resembled shamans and magicians more than Buddhist monks.

*Arupa Loka–* the realm of formlessness, the highest four planes in the Buddhist cosmography.

*Ashoka–* the ideal Buddhist king (272-231 BC).

*asuras–* demons.

*Avici-hell–* the deepest and most horrifying hell of the Buddhist cosmos.

*Ayeyarwady–* also known as Irrawaddy or the Elephant River. It traverses the country for 2,170 kilometers (1,350 miles) and is navigable up to Bhamo and by launches to Myitkyina. Its mother streams are the Mettka and the Malittka, which join about 50 kilometers (30 miles) north of Myitkyina, and its principal tributary is the Chindwinn. The Ayeyarwady enters the delta about 300 kilometers (180 miles) north of the Andaman Sea.

# B

*Bagan–* also known as Pagan, a ruined temple city in Myingyan Province. Founded in AD 847, it became the capital of the First Myanmar Empire in the 11th century. In 1287 it was sacked by Kublai Khan's troops. A third of the city has been swept away by the Ayeyarwady.

*Bagan Era–* the Bagan Era is considered to have begun in AD 638; the year 1355 of the Bagan Era corresponds to the year 1993 of the Christian Era. It was used to calculate time before the Europeans came to the country. There are two more eras known in Myanmar, the Buddhist Era, which began in 544 BC, and the Prome Era starting in AD 78.

*Bago–* also known as Pegu, is the capital of the Bago District. It was founded in AD 825 by immigrants from Orissa in India; its original name was Ussa. In the 16th century it was the capital of the Second Myanmar Empire.

*Bamars–* the Myanmar spelling for Burmans, it refers to the largest and culturally dominant ethnic group.

*Borobudur–* an impressive Buddhist structure in Java.

*Buddha–* "the Enlightened One." Usually it refers to Gautama, who lived in the 5th century BC, though there are 28 Buddhas recognized in Myanmar, and the last one, Mettaya, is yet to come.

# C

*cakkavatti–* a Universal Monarch, literally, "the turner of the wheel."

*chedi–* the same as a stupa, a domelike mound housing relics.

*Chettyars–* an Indian professional caste of moneylenders who demanded a 12 percent-a-month interest rate. They owned half of the fertile land in the country. After independence most of them were expelled.

*Chins–* a Tibeto-Burman ethnolinguistic group that lives in Chin State in the northwest of the country.

# D

*Dagon–* ancient name of Yangon.

*Dawei–* a district and city in Tanintharyi, also known as Tavoy.

*Deva Loka–* the heavens above the seven mountains that surround Mount Meru.

*dhamma–* the teaching of the Buddha.

*dhammaraja–* a king who defends and propagates Buddhist doctrine.

*dhammathat–* an ancient law book that remains the basis of today's civil law in Myanmar.

*Dhammazedi–* (1472-1492) king of Bago, a very pious king who sent monks to Sri Lanka to obtain a valid Theravada ordination. On their return they ordained the Myanmar clergy and attained thereby a measure of unity in the *sangha* that was unknown before.

162

*Dhannavati*– a kingdom in Rakhine that flourished between the 6th century BC and AD 350.

*dukkha*– suffering in Pali.

**F** ● · · · · · · · · · · · · · · · · · · · · · · · · · · · · · · ·

*First Anglo-Burmese War*– (1823-1826) it started with the Myanmars attacking a British outpost across the Naaf estuary and ended with the Treaty of Yandabo in which the Myanmars ceded the coastal provinces of Rakhine and Tanintharyi to Britain.

**G** ● · · · · · · · · · · · · · · · · · · · · · · · · · · · · · · ·

*Gansu*– province in northwest China.

*Gaur*– an ancient kingdom in Bengal.

*Gautama*– name of the last Buddha.

**H** ● · · · · · · · · · · · · · · · · · · · · · · · · · · · · · · ·

*Hamsawaddy*– the ancient name of Bago (Pegu), named after the mythological duck, Brahma's riding vehicle.

**IJ** ● · · · · · · · · · · · · · · · · · · · · · · · · · · · · · · ·

*Innwa*– ruined city, 10 kilometers (6 miles) southwest of Mandalay, also known as Ava. It was founded in 1364 and was the capital of Myanmar until 1783 and again between 1823 and 1837.

*Jambudipa*– the island where the rose-apple tree grows, the southernmost of the islands surrounding Mount Meru, it is the home of man. Only here can future Buddhas be born.

*Jataka stories*– the birth stories of the Buddha, 547 of which are known in the Buddhist world; in Myanmar, however, three more were added.

**K** ● · · · · · · · · · · · · · · · · · · · · · · · · · · · · · · ·

*Kachins*– a Tibeto-Burman ethnolinguistic group. They live in Kachin State and are also known as Jingpaws.

*Kama Loka*– the realm of the sensuous world, which consists of 11 different planes; on one of them lives man.

*kamma*– good or bad deeds in former lives that influence one's present situation.

*kammaraja*– a king who builds temples and stupas to gain merits for himself and his people.

*Karen*– since 1989 their official name is *Kayin*. They belong to a Sino-Tibetan ethnolinguistic group. They live in the Ayeyarwady delta area and in the hills bordering Thailand. The *Pwo Karen* are plain dwellers while the *Kayah* live in Kayah State and the *Pa O* in Shan State. The *Sgaw* and *Pwo* are also called *White Karen*.

*Konbaung-Dynasty*– the last Myanmar dynasty before the British annexed the country and sent the last king, Thibaw, into exile to India.

*Kublai Khan*– the Mongol ruler of China who sacked Bagan in 1287.

*Kyanzittha*– king of the Bagan Dynasty (1084-1112). He was a son of Anawrahta and is remembered as the builder of the Ananda Temple.

*kyaung*– a Buddhist monastery and a school where children learn to read, write and calculate, as well as the basics of the religion.

**L** ● · · · · · · · · · · · · · · · · · · · · · · · · · · · · · · ·

*Lahu*– a Tibeto-Burman ethnolinguistic group that lives mainly along the Yunnan-Myanmar border.

**M** ● · · · · · · · · · · · · · · · · · · · · · · · · · · · · · · ·

*Maghs*– Rakhinese pirates and slave traders who plundered the coast of Rakhine between the 16th and the 18th centuries.

*Maha Muni*– one of Buddhism's most sacred images. After conquering Rakhine in 1785, King Bodawpaya brought it to Amarapura where it is now, together with other spoils of war, in the Maha Muni Pagoda.

*Mahayana Buddhism*– the "Great Vehicle" in which a *boddhisatva* assists laymen on their way to salvation.

*Manu*– ancient Indian law giver.

*Manuha*– the Mon king of *Thaton*, who was brought together with 30,000 artisans to Bagan. There he first lived in Myinkaba close to Bagan and had several important temples built. Later, he and his family were made pagoda slaves at the Shwezigon Pagoda in Nyaung U.

*Mara*– the ruler of *Kama Loka*, the god of sensuality.

*Mawlamyine*– large city at the mouth of the Thanlwin (Salween) also known as Moulmein. During the British period it was an important trade center.

*Mindon Min*– an enlightened king of the Konbaung Dynasty (1853-1878). He is the founder of Mandalay and hosted the Fifth Great Synod of Buddhism in 1872.

*Mons*– a lowland Mon-Khmer ethnolinguistic group of Mongoloid stock. They live mainly in the northern portion of the Tanintharyi panhandle. They were already settled in the country before the Myanmars came.

*Mount Meru*– the center of the world in Buddhist cosmology. Indians still climb up to the foot of Mount Kailas in southwestern Tibet, which for them is Mount Meru.

***Myanmar*** – the new official name of what was known as *Burma*. It derives from the Chinese name *Mien*, the Shans called it *Man* and there exists an 11th century Talaing inscription where it was called *Mirma*.

**N** ••••••••••••••••••••••••••••

***Naga cult*** – an ancient animistic cult around a sacred five headed snake, images of which are still to be found on pagoda arches.

***nat*** – a spirit or god.

***nibbana*** – "extinction," the goal of every Buddhist, when the cycle of rebirths ceases.

**O** ••••••••••••••••••••••••••••

***Ogre*** – man-eating giant.

***Okkala*** – ancient name of Yangon.

***Okkalapa*** – king of Okkala, the region where the Shwedagon was built.

**P** ••••••••••••••••••••••••••••

***Pali*** – a dialect of the Prakrit region in India, in which Gautama's teachings were written down. The sacred language of the Theravadins.

***papaver somniferum*** – opium.

***Pathein*** – also known as Bassein, an Ayeyarwady delta city that is accessible by large steamers. It is a rice-milling and export center.

***paya kywan*** – a hereditary bonded pagoda slave.

***pongyi*** – an ordained Buddhist monk attached to a particular monastery.

***ponnas*** – Brahmins who prescribed the king's activities according to ancient Hindu manuals on kingcraft. Some are still serving the king of Thailand.

***pretas*** – ghosts or specters.

***Pubbavideha*** – the easternmost island in the Buddhist cosmos.

***Pyay*** – also known as Prome, is one of the oldest cities of Myanmar. It was founded in the 8th century by the Pyu.

***Pyin-U-Lwin*** – a hill station, 60 kilometers (42 miles) from Mandalay, it is also known as Maymyo. It was the government summer capital during the British period.

***Pyu*** – they inhabited the Ayeyarwady river valley before the Bamars came. Their most important center was Sri Ksetra close to the city of Pyay. In AD 822 their culture was destroyed by an invasion from Nan-chao. Today they do not exist any more as a distinct people.

**R** ••••••••••••••••••••••••••••

***Rakhine*** – also known as Arakan, the Myanmar state along the Bay of Bengal.

***Rakhine Yoma*** – the mountain range that divides Myanmar proper from the coastal strip of Rakhine.

***Ramanadesa*** – the land of the Ramans.

***Ramans*** – what the Mons once called themselves.

***Rohingyas*** – the Muslim population of Rakhine.

***rupa*** – the material elements of a sentient being.

***Rupa Loka*** – the 16 levels of the realm of subtle material matter in the Buddhist cosmology.

**S** ••••••••••••••••••••••••••••

***samanera*** – a Buddhist novice.

***samsara*** – the wheel of rebirth. The doctrine that says all creatures are involved in an endless cycle of existence, birth, death and rebirth.

***Sanda-thu-dhamma*** – 17th century Rakhine king.

***sangha*** – the fraternity or order of Buddhist monks.

***sangharaja*** – a king who protects and supports the order of the monks.

***Sanskrit Buddhism*** – another word for Mahayana Buddhism. Contrary to the Theravada scriptures, the canon of Mahayana Buddhism was written down in Sanskrit and not in Pali.

***sawbwa*** – a hereditary Shan prince.

***sayadaw*** – a learned and revered elder Buddhist monk, the presiding monk over a monastery.

***Saya San*** – an ex-monk who claimed to be in possession of magical powers and the head of the Tharrawaddy Rebellion in the 1930s. During the rebellion 10,000 rebels were killed by the British Indian army and 9,000 were taken prisoner. 128 of these were later hanged, including Saya San.

***Second Anglo-Burmese War*** – (1851-1852) it started when the kings Tharrawaddy and Pagan Min refused to honor the Treaty of Yandabo (signed at the end of the First Anglo-Burmese War) and ended with the annexation of Yangon, Pathein, Bago and Prome.

***Schah Shuja*** – brother of Aurangzeb and rightful heir to the Mogul throne.

***Shaivism*** – the worship of Shiva.

***Shans*** – a western Thai ethnolinguistic group who call themselves *Tai Yai* if they live in the northern part of the Shan state and *Tai Tau* if they come from the southern part of the state. They are predominantly Buddhist but hold a variety of occult beliefs and practices.

***Shin Arahan*** – a monk from *Thaton* who influenced Anawrahta, Kyanzittha and Alaungsithu to adopt Theravada Buddhism as the state's religion. He died around AD 1115 at the age of 81.

*shin-pyu* – the Buddhist initiation ceremony for boys before they become monks.

*Shinsawbu* – queen of Bago (1453-1472), the only woman who has ever ruled Myanmar. She gave the Shwedagon its present appearance.

*Shwedagon Pagoda* – believed to have been built in 585 BC. It is situated on Singuttara Hill, the last hill of the Bago Range. It rises nearly 100 meters (326 feet) above the platform and is covered all over with gold leaf and gold plate.

*Shwezigon Pagoda* – begun by Anawrahta in 1059 and completed by Kyanzittha. One of Myanmar's most venerated pagodas in the vicinity of Bagan; in a shack beside it are the images of the 37 national nats.

*SLORC* – the *State Law and Order Restoration Council* which took power in September 1988.

*Sokkate* – ruler of Bagan who was slain by Anawrahta in 1044.

*stream enterer* – one who will be reborn on a higher plane of existence.

*stupa* – a dome-like mound. The main Buddhist monument seen all over Myanmar. It developed from the burial mounds of Buddhist kings or saints but represents also the Buddhist universe. Other names are *chedi* or *zedi*.

*Suvannabhumi* – "the land of Gold," the Mons' ancient settlement area along the Malay peninsula.

 **. . . . . . . . . . . . . . . . . . . . . . . . . . .**

*T'ang era* – Chinese dynasty between the 7th and the 10th centuries when art and literature flourished.

*Talaings* – literally means people from Telingana in South India. A name given to the Mon people of South Myanmar.

*Tanintharyi* – also known as Tenasserim, the southern panhandle of Myanmar. It often changed hands between the Siamese and the Myanmars.

*Tantra Buddhism* – a mystical form of Buddhism.

*tatmadaw* – the military, which sees itself as the vanguard of the Myanmar people.

*tazaung* – a pavilion on a pagoda platform.

*Thadingyut* – month around September/October.

*Thamaing* – the legendary and authentic history of a pagoda. Very often it is written in verse form.

*Thanlwin* – also known as Salween, this river is 2,850 kilometers (1,750 miles) long and flows along the border with Thailand and through deep gorges to Mawlamyine where it empties into the Gulf of Martaban.

*Thaton* – the ancient capital of the Mon kingdom which was conquered by Anawrahta.

*Theravada Buddhism* – "the Way of the Elders," the original Pali version of the Buddha's religion. In the 3rd century BC it spread from India to Sri Lanka and from there all over Southeast Asia.

*Theravadin* – disciple of Theravada Buddhism.

*Thibaw* – the last king of Myanmar (1878-1885). When coming to power he massacred his kinsmen. General Prendergast, who entered Mandalay on November 29, 1885, gave him just 45 minutes to pack and disappear into exile.

*Thiri-thu-dhamma* – king of Rakhine (1622-1638).

*Tipitaka scriptures* – the three baskets into which the Theravada canon is divided. The *sutta-pitaka* contains the discourses of the Buddha, the *vinaya-pitaka* the rules of the order and the *abhidhamma-pitaka* an analysis of the scriptures.

 **. . . . . . . . . . . . . . . . . . . . . . . . . . .**

*Uttakuru* – the northernmost island of the Buddhist cosmos.

 **. . . . . . . . . . . . . . . . . . . . . . . . . . .**

*Vaishnavism* – the worship of Vishnu.

 **. . . . . . . . . . . . . . . . . . . . . . . . . . .**

*yadaya* – a medieval magical art, comprised of incantations and sounds at predetermined times and places intended to drive enemies from the country.

*Yangon* – also known as Rangoon, the capital of Myanmar. It was given its present name by Alaungpaya, the founder of the last Myanmar dynasty, signifying "the end of strife."

*Yunnan* – province in southwest China which was independent until 1253. It was then called *Nan-chao* and inhabited by Chinese Shans who migrated south and populated much of Myanmar and Thailand.

*zawgyi* – a magician or sorcerer.

166

*The numbers on the map mark the regions where the pictures in this book were taken.*

*They refer to the following chapters:*

The content of the first chapter, *Landscapes of the Mind*, covers all of Myanmar (and the mythical worlds beyond), therefore it is not specially marked on the map.

No. **2** refers to the ancient *Arimaddana*, today's *Bagan*.

No. **3** marks *Mandalay* and the ancient cities in its vicinity, *Amarapura*, *Innwa (Ava)* and *Sagaing*.

No. **4** marks *Rakhine*, the Myanmar state at the Bay of Bengal. Pfannmüller's photographs were taken in the vicinity of *Myohaung*.

No. **5** marks the southern *Shan-hills*. The photographs were taken in the region around *Lake Inle*.

No. **6** marks *Southern Myanmar*. Pfannmüller's photographs were taken in *Yangon*, the delta of the *Ayeyarwady*, in *Bago (Pegu)* and at the *Golden Rock*.